I STAND AT THE DOOR AND KNOCK

ALSO OF INTEREST

Reflections of God's Glory by Corrie ten Boom
Messages of God's Abundance by Corrie ten Boom
The Five Silent Years of Corrie ten Boom
by Pamela Rosewell Moore

I STAND AT THE DOOR AND KNOCK

CORRIE ten BOOM

Z ZONDERVAN®

ZONDERVAN.com/
AUTHORTRACKER
follow your favorite authors

ZONDERVAN®

I Stand at the Door and Knock
Copyright © 2008 by Stichting Trans World Radio Voor Nederland en Belgie

This title is also available in a Zondervan downloadable
audio edition. Visit www.zondervan.fm.

This title is also available as a Zondervan ebook.
Visit www.zondervan.com/ebooks.

Requests for information should be addressed to:

Zondervan, *Grand Rapids, Michigan 49530*

Library of Congress Cataloging-in-Publication Data

Ten Boom, Corrie.
    I stand at the door and knock : meditations by the author of The hiding place/
Corrie ten Boom.
        p. cm.
        ISBN 978-0-310-27154-3 (hardcover)
    1. Christian life—Meditations. I. Title.
    BV4501.3.T453 2008
    242—dc22

2008009758

Interior design by Michelle Espinoza

Printed in the United States of America

---

08 09 10 11 12 13 14 • 22 21 20 19 18 17 16 15 14 13 12 11 10 9 8 7 6 5 4 3 2 1

CONTENTS

FOREWORD

Pretend for a moment that you are sitting beside your radio in your quaint home in the Netherlands in 1966. It has now been more than two decades since the German occupation of your homeland in World War II. Yet the scars of those dark days are still evident all around you. Many mothers and fathers lost their sons in battle. Many Jews—grandparents, parents, and even children—who played a prominent part in the life of the country were literally exterminated en masse during the Holocaust occurring under Adolf Hitler's reign. And many Jewish sympathizers—those who believed in standing against wrong no matter what the cost—were interred in concentration camps and lost their lives as they stood and chose to suffer alongside their Jewish friends and neighbors.

Such was the plight of the Ten Boom family of Haarlem, the Netherlands. A devoutly Christian family, they harbored, fed, and cared for Jews in their home who would have otherwise been destined for the concentration camps. Their story is chronicled in one of the bestselling Christian books of our time, *The Hiding Place*—referring to the secret place where the Ten Booms hid Jews, a story that went on to become a major motion picture.

On February 28, 1944, the lives of the Ten Boom family changed forever. On that day, Corrie, her watchmaker father, her older sister, Betsie, and thirty-five other people were arrested for not disclosing the whereabouts of six Jews hidden in a secret room attached to her bedroom. Corrie's father died within ten days of his arrest, while Corrie and Betsie were imprisoned and subjected to the atrocities of the Ravensbrück concentration camp in Germany. Corrie survived the experience, her release from Ravensbrück later determined to be due to a clerical error shortly before all women her age were to be executed. Betsie, however, died at Ravensbrück.

Perhaps the greatest scars resulting from the Holocaust were the scars of bitterness and unforgiveness that destroyed many more lives. Corrie struggled with these same feelings herself. Yet through God's amazing work in her life, she became a worldwide symbol of reconciliation, forgiveness, and the ultimate hope found in Christ as she wrote nine books, spoke in more than sixty countries, and produced five films as part of her ministry to lost and hurting people—a ministry that didn't begin until she was in her fifties. When lists have been compiled of the greatest Christians of the twentieth century, Corrie's name is commonly included and often near the top.

"That's her voice now," you say to yourself as you turn on your radio and hear Corrie's unmistakable voice speaking in her native Dutch. You're now hearing some of the first devotional messages by Corrie that were commonly aired to the Netherlands from 1966 through the early 1970s by Trans World Radio (www.twr.org), the world's most far-reaching international Christian radio broadcasting ministry.

In fact, the book you are now holding will most likely be the final chapter in the four decades that Corrie's ministry and that of TWR have been inextricably interwoven. It represents the third and final book in a series of Corrie's "lost" devotional messages that she broadcast over TWR, following *Reflections of God's Glory* (1999) and *Messages of God's Abundance* (2002), both books also published by Zondervan. How this book came about is a story in itself.

In 1996, on my way back from meetings in eastern Europe, I made my first stopover at TWR's office in the Netherlands, then located in Voorthuizen. One of the reasons for my visit was curiosity over some written scripts of Corrie ten Boom's radio messages that one of my colleagues had told me about. As I inquired about these Dutch scripts, I was astounded to discover that no one in the office thought they had ever been translated into English before and published, although some of them had been published in Dutch. This began a six-year odyssey of translating various radio messages and then doing extensive research to determine if they had been published elsewhere — resulting in the publishing of the first two books featuring twenty-four and twenty-six messages, respectively.

We thought we were through — but God had another plan! I was contacted late last year by Zondervan expressing interest in publishing a new compendium version of the two books and inquiring as to whether we had any more materials that had not been included earlier that could be added to the new volume.

I was quite sure that we had no more new materials, as all of the written scripts were the result of an exhaustive search over a decade ago. I decided, however, to inquire of our staff in the Netherlands, especially TWR missionary Claire Rothrock, without whose faithful and tireless work these three books would not have been possible. A few days later, I received an excited phone call from Claire. It appeared she had found some new materials — not just a few, but many! While all along we had assumed that our audio archives were a duplication of the written scripts, Claire discovered that there were in fact forty new messages for which no written scripts existed.

As I was doing a final edit on these messages, what impressed me once again is what I would call the "profound simplicity" of Corrie's words. It is a job truly to be approached as if walking on holy ground — so anointed was the ministry that God gave to Corrie. Now you too can put yourself into the shoes of that post–World War II radio listener in the Netherlands. We have transcribed and translated these materials just as Corrie wrote them — which is why you will read occasional references to "radio" or to "the listener" within these pages.

Concidentally, the timing of the publication of this book also marks the twenty-fifth anniversary of Corrie's death. (Corrie died on April 15, 1983, the day of her ninety-first birthday.) Yet I think you will find, as I did in editing this book, that while much history has been written in the last forty years, Corrie's spiritual insights and vivid illustrations remain timelessly refreshing and astoundingly relevant for our times and for how they address the spiritual condition of man. The words that God gave this amazing woman continue to speak powerfully and piercingly into our lives, and TWR and Zondervan are pleased to once again bring alive these words to a new generation.

Thomas M. Watkins
U.S. Director, Strategic Initiatives
& Partnerships, Trans World Radio
Cary, North Carolina
April 2008

I STAND AT THE DOOR
AND KNOCK

I Stand at the Door and Knock

Let's talk about how you and I can be used for a revival, and how to be the light of the world in these times.

I am always touched by the story of a woodpecker who tapped its beak against a tree trunk, and the moment it did so a flash of lightning struck the tree and totally demolished it. The woodpecker flew away and said to the other birds, "I didn't know there was such incredible power in my beak."

You see, if you and I want to be used, we needn't rely on ourselves, because it is the Holy Spirit who does it. And that is why we can be at peace in our day-to-day lives. The fact that we wish to be used is a gift from the Holy Spirit in itself. It is necessary that the world knows that death is the wage of sin. But the grace given by God is eternal life in Jesus Christ, our Lord.

Do you understand? I understood very little, until I reached a difficult period in the school of life. You learn a lot during difficult times. It was when I was a prisoner in a German concentration camp named Ravensbrück, and I was interrogated by a judge, who would decide my fate. It was during World War II. And the Lord gave me an opportunity to talk about the Lord. The man became a friend instead of an enemy. Then he showed me terribly dangerous letters, which could be my death sentence, and also hurt my family and friends. He knew how dangerous they were. Suddenly he threw them into the fire. And when I saw those flames consume the incredibly dangerous papers, for the first time I understood what was written in Colossians 2:14, that the record of our sin was taken away by Jesus and nailed to the cross.

You see, that's when I began to understand that eternal life is given by God, by the Lord Jesus Christ. Maybe some will say, "I don't understand. What do I need to do to receive it?" Jesus said, "No one can see the kingdom of God unless he is born again" (John 3:3). And He also said, "Come to me, all you who are weary and burdened, and I will give you rest" (Matthew 11:28).

In Laodicea were Christians who would say to each other, "I am rich, and I lack nothing," but one thing was missing, something very important—they had locked the Lord Jesus out of their hearts. And then the Lord said to them, "I stand at the door and knock. If anyone hears my voice and opens the door, I will come in" (Revelation 3:20). If you ask Jesus to come into your heart, He will enter. And He will perform the miracle that you are born into the family of God.

The Bible says, "Yet to all who received him, to those who believed in his name, he gave the right to become children of God" (John 1:12). That is when you can say to God, "Father, my Father." And He will say to you, "My child." This is so very important, that when it happens, the angels rejoice, because you are invaluable in God's eyes. When Jesus enters your heart, you will notice that you need a spring cleaning. And now you may confess all your sins. Whoever confesses their sins and relies on Jesus' power will be saved through His blood.

I went to America this year. One woman was listening very attentively. But when I said, "Do you want to accept Jesus as your Savior?" she said, "I would love to, but I can't."

I understood her distress. She had been a soothsayer. You see, there are sins that entail bondage, causing the Devil to gain and keep you in his power. In these days, there are so many sins of the occult, also in Christian circles. And the people don't know why they are in darkness. It is very clear in Deuteronomy 18:10–13: "Let no one be found among you ... who practices divination or sorcery, interprets omens, engages in witchcraft, or casts spells, or who is a medium or spiritist or who consults the dead. Anyone who does these things is detestable to the LORD, and because of these detestable practices the LORD your God will drive out those nations before you. You must be blameless before the LORD your God."

You see, these things are detestable in God's eyes, because they are ways of asking the Devil to help you. All those things — soothsaying, spiritism, horoscopes — they all belong to the Devil. But the wonderful thing is that though the Devil's power is great, his power is limited, while Jesus' power is unlimited. And that's why we simply need to lay our sins before Him, and then yes, the Lord will forgive us and make us free.

I once stood face-to-face with death. Not once, but very often when I was in prison. And now I have experienced Jesus putting me on victorious ground. Do you need liberating? Are you bound by the sin of the occult? Ask for forgiveness. Send the power of darkness away in Jesus' name. And surrender to the Lord Jesus and serve Him. His yoke is easy; His burden is light.

I have worked in sixty-three countries, where I have told people about the Lord Jesus. And I've never met anybody who said that they were sorry that the Lord Jesus had entered their hearts. And you won't regret it either if you surrender to Him.

Thank You, Lord Jesus, that we can rely on You. Because You have said, "Come to me, all of you." And that includes those who have been listening just now. Thank You, that You love him, that You love her, and that You love me so deeply! Hallelujah! Amen.

JESUS LOVES SINNERS

John 7:37–39 says, "On the last and greatest day of the Feast, Jesus stood and said in a loud voice, 'If anyone is thirsty, let him come to me and drink. Whoever believes in me, as the Scripture has said, streams of living water will flow from within him.' By this he meant the Spirit, whom those who believed in him were to receive later."

Jesus called, "Come." He didn't say it softly, so that only the people close to Him could hear it. He said it loudly so that they could all hear it, and He is saying it to you too, through the radio, "Come."

"Oh," you may say, "that could be something for others, for my respectable neighbor, who goes to church so regularly and is so decent, but it's not for me, because I am too sinful. No, I wouldn't dare to. Oh, no, becoming religious is not for me; I am much too bad for that." Look, if you say that now, Jesus is precisely what is needed.

There was only one sort of person whom the Lord Jesus did not accept when He said, "Come." They are the ones who said to Him, "Yes, here I am, Jesus, and I'm very good and very virtuous." Some of them were called Pharisees. To them the Lord Jesus said, "Are you very virtuous? Then I am sorry, but I can't help you."

If such a Pharisee were to say, "In other people's eyes I am virtuous, but there is sin in my heart," then the Lord Jesus would say, "Then come to me, I'm going to help you." If you now say, "I am too bad to come to Jesus," then you are exactly the person He wants to help and is able to help. So just come!

Jesus loves sinners. He only loves sinners. He has never turned anyone away who came to Him for forgiveness, and He died on the cross for sinners, not for respectable people. It was exactly for sinners that He suffered so terribly on the cross, so much so that it was almost impossible for Him to bear. So dreadful, that He said, "My God, my God, why have you forsaken me?" (Mark 15:34). He did all that for sinners like you, so just come.

And then when you come to Him, He will deliver you from your sins. But you also have to confess them and bring them to Him. If you look to Jesus in His great love, if you look at Him in faith, then you will be ashamed of yourself, then you'll pray, "Oh Lord, be merciful to me, a sinner." And do you know what is so wonderful? He is merciful to sinners and you can take your sins to Him now. You can say, "Lord, that is so wrong, and I said that, and thought that," and if you then confess that, it's just as if a great weight falls from your shoulders.

In that wonderful, classic book *The Pilgrim's Progress* by John Bunyan, Pilgrim arrives at the cross, and the heavy burden of his sins on his back falls from him. That is the reality if you come to Jesus; the burden of sin will fall from you. You can confess them to Him; you may and you must confess them to Him. And it's not just that you confess them, but you repent of them. John says, "If we confess our sins, he is faithful and just and will forgive us our sins and purify us from all unrighteousness" (1 John 1:9).

Look! You haven't just confessed your sins, but the great miracle takes place in your life when Jesus cleanses you with His blood. Yes, what's that? The blood of Jesus? I can't understand it either, but I know that it works. You see, I also know what it points to. Jesus gave His blood on the cross to purchase you and me. A terrible, heavy, and expensive price. If you speak of the blood of Jesus, you think of the completed work on the cross. But, as it says in the Bible, if you bring your sins to Jesus now, He will forgive you, and He will cast your sins into the depths of the sea.

I think there should be a sign saying "No fishing," because the Devil likes to make things difficult for you about all these sins that have been confessed. But sins which have been brought to the Lord are dead. It says that He removes our sin from us as far as the east is from the west. He makes them disappear, just as a cloud disappears. Now, if a cloud disappears it never comes back. Then the Lord gives you His Spirit in your heart, with the fruit of the Spirit. Just the opposite of your sins. Love, joy, goodness.

Won't you be tempted anymore? Yes, of course. The Devil definitely won't leave you alone, but now I can recommend a wonderful habit, and that is to bring your sins to the Lord immediately. You need to do that immediately, because otherwise the Devil will accuse you. It says in the Bible that he accuses the children of God day and night. But it's so wonderful that if you've brought them to the Lord, even if it's just two minutes before the Devil comes to accuse you, you have nothing to fear. Then the Lord will say, "I have already cast these sins into the depths of the sea; they are gone." So the Devil has nothing left to say.

Thank You, Lord Jesus, for coming to save sinners, to make them joyful, to set them free. To give them peace instead of discord. Thank You that those today who have understood that for the first time may also come, that You stretch out Your hand to them and say, "Come." Lord, did you see that? Of course You saw it! You heard when they said, "Yes, I come, Lord Jesus." Oh, how wonderful, Lord, that now You are going to do that wonderful thing in their lives, that they stand firm in the battle. That You will make them more than conquerors, that You will fill them with Your Holy Spirit. Thank You, Lord Jesus, that You make sinners happy, that You deliver them. Hallelujah, what a Savior! Amen.

3

What Can I Do about My Sins?

D ear fellow sinners, I have a message for you. The Devil is like a good cattle merchant who walks around a cow once to inspect it and then knows all its weaknesses. He knows you and me, and he knows exactly where he can hurt us. The Devil has not retired yet. He knows his time is short, and he is very active.

In the concentration camp I lived near a crematorium for months. I was living in the shadow of death. I did not know beforehand that they would release me a week before they would kill all the women my age. It was a human error and a miracle of God.

When you face eternity, and that was what was happening to me, you see everything so clearly. Here I was weak and sinful, and there was the Devil, much stronger than me, much, much stronger than me. But there was Jesus, much, much stronger than the Devil. And together with Him, I was more than a conqueror.

And that provides the right answer to our problem with sin. Jesus said, "I have not come to call the righteous, but sinners" (Matthew 9:13). What should we do? Proverbs 28:13 tells us, "He who conceals his sins does not prosper, but whoever confesses and renounces them finds mercy." Do not cover up, but confess and stop sinning. "If we confess our sins, he is faithful and just and will forgive us our sins and purify us from all unrighteousness," says 1 John 1:9.

A man in a small village once visited a priest. He asked him if he could confess his sin and if he could have absolution. "I stole three sacks of potatoes," he said.

The priest listened and talked about repentance and forgiveness. When the conversation was finished, the priest said, "I heard about the theft of those bags of potatoes, but I heard that it concerned only two, and you mentioned three."

"Yes," said the man, "but tomorrow I will steal the third."

Whoever confesses their sins should stop committing them. When Jesus revealed His unprecedented great mercy for sinners towards the woman who had committed adultery, He said, "If any one of you is without sin, let him be the first to throw a stone at her" (John 8:7). And all the people He spoke to walked away. Then the Lord said to the sinful woman, "Go now and leave your life of sin" (John 8:11).

You might say, "That's all good and well the Lord saying sin no more, but I regard it as a high mountain peak, as the summit on which I will never be able to stand." But you know what is so wonderful? When you climb with the Lord

Jesus, you see that it is a high plateau, not a mountaintop. And you experience Psalm 18:36 where a sinner speaks to the Lord, "You broaden the path beneath me."

The Bible states it very clearly in Jeremiah 3:13, "Only acknowledge your guilt — you have rebelled against the LORD your God." And what about the wonderful words in Isaiah 1:18, " 'Come now, let us reason together,' says the LORD. 'Though your sins are like scarlet, they shall be as white as snow; though they are red as crimson, they shall be like wool.' "

Jesus died on the cross to save sinners, and whoever Jesus makes free is truly free. When the Devil shows us our sins, it is only to make us desperate. "That is what you are like," he says, "and that is how you will be the rest of your life." But when the Holy Spirit shows us our sins, it is always in the light of the completed work on the cross where Jesus died for you and for me. He did not only die for us. He lives! And He is with us, now and forever.

A three-year-old little boy once went to meet his father at the train. "I want to carry your suitcase, Daddy," he said.

"Good lad," said his father. "Put your hand on my hand." Together, they carried the heavy suitcase.

When they arrived home the little lad told his mother, "I carried Daddy's heavy suitcase."

And that is exactly what we should do. Lay our weak hand in Jesus' strong hand. We are strong together with Him. Yes, more than conquerors. You and I will not be silly and say, "I carried the suitcase." We will praise and glorify Him, who not only helps us carry our burdens, but carries us too. "For God did not give us a spirit of timidity, but a spirit of power, of love and of self-discipline" (2 Timothy 1:7).

> *Thank You, Lord Jesus, that Your answer to our problem over sin is so wonderful and clear. Thank You that You have said, "Come to me, all you who are weary and burdened, and I will give you rest." Thank You. Hallelujah, what a Savior! Amen.*

BLAMELESS AND SPOTLESS

I can be so happy when I contemplate that the Lord Jesus will return again very soon. But sometimes I am so afraid. Do you feel that way too? Then I think of the foolish virgins who weren't ready, who didn't have enough oil in their lamps, and who didn't get to the wedding banquet. Yes, sometimes I feel like one of the wise virgins. But then doubting again, afraid and weak, I change like the weather in April. So active and happy today, quiet and indifferent tomorrow. But once Jesus arrives, the two of us will win, Jesus and me. Yes, Jesus and me, together.

I understand that when He returns, we will have to be at peace with God and other people. Second Peter 3:14 says, "So then, dear friends, since you are looking forward to this, make every effort to be found spotless, blameless and at peace with him." At peace. How is that possible? That you and I have to be blameless and spotless? But it is possible. The problem of sin has an answer, on the cross.

There is still a battle here, not against flesh and blood but against the spiritual forces from Satan's headquarters. The Holy Spirit convicts us of sin, and we have to listen. The accuser, the liar, Satan, convicts us of sin too if he can manage to do that, and then we listen to him. He then says, "Can't you see, that's just how you are. That's typically your character; you'll stay like this for the rest of your life." That just makes you desperate.

I was fighting a battle with the sin of worrying, permitting a real spirit of worry. It looked very much like unbelief. Lack of confidence. Yes, I know that being anxious is a sin. And the Enemy said, "Look, that's just like you. Don't you remember, then and then, you did it then too. You're bound to stay like this; it's part of your character."

Then I sent him away, and I started talking to the Lord. I told Him everything. The Holy Spirit said to me, "Yes, it was wrong of you to do that, being worried is unbelief, and unbelief is sin. But Jesus died on the cross for that sin, and He accomplished everything that needed to be done." And then I picked up my Bible and read those wonderful, radical answers.

Oh, if you start searching the Bible, you receive such wonderful answers. He throws our sin over His shoulders. He casts them into the depths of the sea. He removes them as far as the east is from the west. If you confess your sins, He is faithful and just to forgive you your sins, and the blood of Jesus Christ cleanses us of all sin. Actually, confession becomes a wonderful experience, just as you are grateful for a good bath. If the blood of Jesus cleanses you, well, that is peace.

But now, to be at peace with my fellow human beings—that is often a problem for me. Usually people are so good and friendly towards me, but sometimes ... And then having to forgive! To forgive just as we expect the Lord to forgive us. Jesus said that if we don't do it, we won't receive forgiveness ourselves, so we have to. If you don't forgive, you break the bridge—the same bridge that you need as well.

Remember the wonderful promise in Romans 5:5, "And hope does not disappoint us, because God has poured out his love into our hearts by the Holy Spirit, whom he has given us." God's love is the answer, and we give thanks for it. Have you had trouble with forgiving? Pray this prayer, which was the solution for me.

Thank You, Lord, for Romans 5:5. Thank You, Lord Jesus, that You put God's love in my heart through the Holy Spirit, which was given to me. Thank You, Father, that Your love in me is stronger than my anger toward those who treated me so cruelly. And it always works. Yes, thank You, Lord Jesus, that You wish to prepare us for Your return. That You want to make us blameless and spotless, if we put our weak hand calmly in Your hand, and I do that now. Amen.

HOW OFTEN SHOULD I FORGIVE?

Seventy times seven. That is how often we need to forgive. I can't believe it; how is that possible? Because you yourself have received forgiveness more than seventy times seven. He warned us in Matthew 6:14–15, "For if you forgive men when they sin against you, your heavenly Father will also forgive you." Therefore, we should forgive, and then your heavenly Father will do the same with your sin.

Isn't it wonderful that in His Word the Father uses expressions such as "as far as the east is from the west, so far has he removed our transgressions from us" (Psalm 103:12). He makes them disappear like a cloud. Isn't that wonderful, because a cloud will never return.

But how will we manage to forgive likewise? A piece of good advice is to forgive anyone immediately—and I mean *immediately*—if they say or do something against you. Then the Devil won't have a chance to keep a shadow in your heart.

I believe that Romans 5:5 gives us the key to forgiveness: "God has poured out his love into our hearts by the Holy Spirit, whom he has given us." That godly love knows how to forgive. It will also succeed in your heart and mine. Be filled with God's Spirit and the fruits of the Spirit, and His love will be so much stronger than annoyance, indignation, or hatred. It means forgiving, forgetting, and loving.

I must admit that I thought it was sufficient to forgive, and I wasn't too bothered about forgetting. I had received letters which contained all kinds of awful things that people had committed against me. I forgave them a long time ago, but then I was reminded what the Lord had done with my sins. They were forgiven and wiped out. Well, that is when I burned all those letters containing the sins of others. And I'm so glad I did! I have experienced that if the Lord Jesus liberates you, you are truly free.

In these days we are being prepared for the kingdom of peace that will come to earth. The Bible is full of promises about what will happen when Jesus returns. The wolf will dwell with the lamb, the swords will be beaten into plowshares, nuclear power will be used to restore, to heal, and no longer to destroy. You might say, "Oh yes, everything will be absolutely wonderful, and it will be easy for me, but the current atmosphere is one of arguing, criticizing, and irritation, particularly among us Christians. And what about our morals; what a lot of cruelty!"

Yes, the world is touched by evil, and the prince of this world is doing his dirty work. Yet in this dark world the Lord Jesus gave us the task of passing on His love. He said, "You are the light of the world" (Matthew 5:14).

Why did God send His Son, Jesus? In order to find and make holy what had been lost! Why does Jesus send you and me? To find what was lost. And it is possible, because He also said, "Peace I leave with you; my peace I give you" (John 14:27). Together with Jesus we will succeed. His love and peace are inexhaustible, and even though it might be difficult, together with Him we are more than conquerors.

Paul stood at the frontline. You can read about it in Acts and in his letters. Didn't he encounter a lot of opposition, hatred, betrayal, slander? In Romans 8:35 he says, "Who shall separate us from the love of Christ? Shall trouble or hardship or persecution or famine or nakedness or danger or sword?" He was in a position to say, "For your sake we face death all day long; we are considered as sheep to be slaughtered" (Romans 8:36). It is not fair, is it? But then he rejoices, "In all these things we are more than conquerors through him who loved us. For I am convinced that neither death nor life, neither angels nor demons, neither the present nor the future, nor any powers, neither height nor depth, nor anything else in all creation, will be able to separate us from the love of God that is in Christ Jesus our Lord" (Romans 8:37–39).

Lord, teach me to forgive everybody immediately, no matter what they have done to me, to burn all their engraved sins. Thank You, that Your peace in my heart is more than sufficient, yes, that it is abundant. Hallelujah! Amen.

6

SOME THOUGHTS ABOUT HOLINESS

"I am not indebted to you, nothing stands between us." This is a greeting in Uganda, Africa.

How do we know in our lives that we have been set apart, have been made holy? By our actions and response. I remember how my sister Betsie really grew in holiness. I once read a letter which said: "Holiness is the Holy Spirit, a holy God in my heart, which makes me similar to Jesus."

The large number of prisoners in the concentration camp always felt like a kind of threat. There were so many criminals among them and everything was so dirty. When you passed through a dense crowd, you always had to knock off the vermin that had settled on your coat. It often frightened me. Once one of those crowds appeared in the street and Betsie said, "I love the crowd." You see, it was a loving response, the Lord Jesus' response in Betsie. She could not have responded in such a way of her own accord. Wanting to be like Him is what had actually happened.

When you come to think of it, you wonder, how can it ever become a reality in me? How can we have such a New-Testament-like experience of holiness? An unconditional surrender is what you need first.

Romans 12:1–2 says: "Therefore, I urge you, brothers, in view of God's mercy, to offer your bodies as living sacrifices, holy and pleasing to God — this is your spiritual act of worship. Do not conform any longer to the pattern of this world, but be transformed by the renewing of your mind. Then you will be able to test and approve what God's will is — his good, pleasing and perfect will."

You see, a potter can only mold the clay when it lies completely in his hand. It requires complete surrender. When the Lord says to us, "Give Me your heart," and we do so, then we need to trust that He will take it. This surrender is not only important when there are great events in our lives, but also in everyday life. My father was a watchmaker. He once said to me, "My name is on my shop, but really God's name should be on the shop, because I am a watchmaker by the grace of God."

When you have surrendered to the Lord, He is with you. He is your Guide, and your Shepherd, forever. I mentioned the word *guide*. An alpine mountaineer, accompanied by a guide, will use the guide when the path is very easy and very straight, but also when it is steep and hazardous. The guide will always be with him on a venture like that.

The same applies to the Lord. He is always with us. Today, while preparing a meal, while writing, while teaching, while doing office work. There might not be any difficulties today. Yes, that is quite possible, but your Guide is with you; the Lord is with you.

We know that when difficulties arise, He will not let us down. I know from experience. I accepted the Lord Jesus when I was five. And He has never let me down! There will be many battles to fight, but one day there will be peace, and we will never be alone in our struggle.

The Holy Spirit can do that, and your secret weapon is your relationship with Jesus and the power of the Holy Spirit. If it is difficult, call on Him. God sanctifies what has been surrendered and committed to Him. We need to surrender to Him, commit ourselves. It can be accomplished by grace. God will do what is necessary to shape you. Otherwise it will never happen.

And when you surrender, God will purify what He takes, and He will empty before He purifies. And then He will fill what He has emptied, and what He has filled, He will use. It means you are living out the Jesus Christ living in you. It doesn't stop at surrender, just like a marriage does not stop at the wedding.

You see, holiness can bring about a new conflict. We need to take care. The Devil wants to lead us into the energy of our inner selves. Preaching yourself, relying on yourself, boasting about your faith, taking pride in your own experiences. And then the Devil will say, "Revel in your own experiences." But that is not right. You should not rely on your past experiences. It may strengthen your faith, but holiness is living out the Jesus Christ living in you. It will become a kind of process of daily surrender. An exercise in faith. A daily exercise in obedience. The Christian who compromises, who has only partly surrendered, will find life really difficult. Nobody can serve two lords.

When you hear this, you might say, "Yes, I can see, but my faith isn't big enough." However, this is not the time to reflect on your faith. You should look at the Lord.

Once I was waiting at a very primitive bridge in New Zealand. We were traveling by car, but we didn't dare to cross. First, one of the men in the car went to investigate if the bridge was strong enough. It appeared to be strong enough, even though it was very primitive, and we crossed without a problem. This man was not investigating our trust in the bridge.

Very often, we tend to look at our faith, and we know our faith is big and strong, or weak and small. But we shouldn't investigate our faith; we should investigate the Bridge. We should not rely on ourselves, but on Him. And when we look to Jesus, we know that He is strong.

The Holy Spirit will not desert you. His peace will reign in your heart. Accepting holiness is a decision. The Lord has selected you for His service. The path is uphill. When you climb a mountain it does not mean that you have reached Mount Everest. It is quite a trek, but it is so wonderful that when we are with Jesus, we are with God.

Lord Jesus, we praise You. And thank You, that You repair our faith when it doesn't work very well, and that You will live in us, that we are in You, that You are in us, which makes us similar. Isn't it wonderful! We thank You for Your Holy Spirit. Hallelujah! Amen.

7

BREAKING THE
VICIOUS CIRCLE

No, don't use that saucer. It is the cat's saucer. You don't use a cat's saucer for yourself, do you? Why not? Because it has been set apart, not for you, but for the cat.

You see, when we have been made holy, we have been set apart by the Lord, for His service and for His honor.

I talk about the importance of holiness because we all need to be ready for Jesus' return. First, if it hasn't happened yet, we need to become a child of God. If we accept Jesus, He authorizes us to become God's child. It is, as Jesus calls it, being born again. You are born into God's kingdom when you invite Jesus into your life, but it is only a start. After that we need to be made holy. First Peter 1:14–16 says, "As obedient children, do not conform to the evil desires you had when you lived in ignorance. But just as he who called you is holy, so be holy in all you do; for it is written: 'Be holy, because I am holy.'"

Holiness is the Holy Spirit's merciful and continuous intervention by which He purifies the sinner, and his entire nature is renewed according to God's image. It enables him to do good deeds. Being made holy is almost like identification. You begin to identify with the Lord Jesus.

Yes, I need to say something else about that word. I'm thinking of those days during the war when the Jews had to wear a yellow star. It was something terrible. It was meant to be the beginning of the end. Afterwards, all the Jews were deported to concentration camps. Father had a great love for the Jews. One day he said, "Please sew a yellow star on my coat." He wanted to identify with the Jews. We didn't, because we knew if we did, he would no longer be able to do anything to help the Jews. He would have been broken along with them.

Identifying means becoming identical. Jesus said, "I am the vine; you are the branches. If a man remains in me and I in him, he will bear much fruit; apart from me you can do nothing" (John 15:5). I believe that an important part of becoming holy is that we need to understand and accept that our sins are forgiven. We often do believe it theologically and theoretically, but it isn't always a reality.

A little girl once broke a beautiful antique cup belonging to her mother. She took it to her mother and she was very upset. Her mother said, "I can see that you are very sorry. I will forgive you. Throw the pieces in the trash."

The next day, the little girl saw the pieces in the trash, and she took them out and took them to her mother. She said, "Mommy, I broke that cup yesterday."

I suspect she loved the experience of forgiveness so much that she wanted to experience it again. But her mother said,

"Leave those pieces in the trash, and just think about my forgiveness."

Don't you and I often feel the same? Not believing in the completed work of forgiveness. Have you ever asked for forgiveness for the same sin again? In that case you are just as silly as that little girl. We need to ask for forgiveness, and then believe we are forgiven. And then we need to turn away from sin, in the power of the Lord.

Turning your back on sin is part of becoming holy. Yes, it is a choice. You and I need to make our own choices. It is God's will to make us holy, but do you love sin too much to turn your back on it? Be careful, death is the wage of sin, whereas God's gift of grace is eternal life.

You see, when you invite the Lord Jesus into your life, and His forgiveness, and you are being made holy through Him, it's as if He lifts you out of a vicious circle. He brings you into a blessed circle. The vicious circle is when you are doing evil things, even though you try very hard not to, and you might temporarily succeed. But you are too weak; you fall down again. The reason is that the Devil is stronger than you. We all experience this. Yes, I really would like to call it a vicious circle. You commit a sin, you repent, you try again, you succeed, and you fail, and then you fall. It simply makes you desperate, that struggle, until you surrender to the Lord Jesus.

Once you surrender, Jesus will lead you like a good Shepherd, who cares for His sheep. The Lord Jesus gave us a beautiful parable: Does He not leave the ninety-nine in the open country and go after the lost sheep until He finds it? He really cares for us, and that is why we needn't despair, when you know that you are one of the good Shepherd's sheep.

The Lord Jesus knew that hell existed. That's why He came down to earth to save you and me from hell. He gave His life to save us, and He warned us. Please read what Jesus said. He was quite clear about it; He said everything very directly.

Now I have spoken about the vicious circle. Lord Jesus places us in a blessed circle, which is a battle against sin, but this time we are together with Somebody who stands on victorious ground. Yes, if you sin, even when you are God's child, and it really upsets you, you will ask for forgiveness. The Lord will cleanse you with His blood, and He will fill you with the Holy Spirit.

Being filled with the Holy Spirit is the complete opposite of sin. Galatians 5:22 says, "But the fruit of the Spirit is love, joy, peace, patience, kindness, goodness, faithfulness, gentleness and self-control." That is how you become holy. It is a wonderful way of becoming holy. And the Holy Spirit is at work in you and me.

Ephesians 6 talks about God's armor. You will see that it is not yet a perfect victory, the final victory. We still need armor, but God's armor is so strong. When you read closely you will see that the Lord Jesus Himself is our armor. He is peace. He is truth. He is in you; you are in Him. It might be a battle, but this time it is in a blessed circle. It is the Devil attacking you; you are falling, but you are lifted up, forgiven, cleansed. That road takes you upward. It becomes increasingly victorious. The Lord Jesus will make you victorious, and you will be more than a conqueror.

Thank You, Lord Jesus, that You lift us out of this vicious circle of sin and failure and that You have brought us into that wonderful blessed circle of forgiveness, redemption, and holiness. Hallelujah, what a Savior. Amen.

8

A Pure and Holy Life

Being made holy is a step toward revival.

Somebody asked the evangelist, Gypsy Smith, "What can I do to achieve revival in my church?"

He replied, "Go to your room, take a piece of chalk, draw a circle on the floor, and kneel down in the center of the circle. And then pray, 'Lord, send a revival to my church, and may it begin in the center of this circle.'"

That was a sharp reply, wasn't it, but he was right. It is God's will that we may become holy. The Lord Jesus clearly said that we needed to be born again, that we can be God's children, and that we will then take our sins to the Lord.

And now I want to speak to the children of God. Anybody can become a child of God, because what was done on the cross has been fulfilled. And all we need to do is say yes to Jesus, with all our heart, and He will perform a miracle so that we become God's children. And that is only the beginning. It is as if we have been set apart in a very special way to be members of Jesus' army.

In Exodus 33:16 Moses asks God, "How will anyone know that you are pleased with me and with your people unless you go with us? What else will distinguish me and your people from all the other people on the face of the earth?" This is about a holy people, and now I'm talking about a holy person. It means that you have found grace in God's eyes, and that He will go with us.

Isn't it wonderful? We will never be alone, no matter what happens. That is why we understand that a Christian who has not become holy, is not part of God's will, but part of God's concern. Please understand that you are not responsible for what you are, but for what you continue to be. Falling into the water doesn't necessarily mean that you will drown, but you will, if you stay in the water.

Being made holy, being cleansed, is about serious truths. There is no room for compromise. Somebody said, "My finger is quite black, but it is still pointing to Jesus." That may be so in the beginning, but it shouldn't continue that way. When you point to Jesus, when you meet Him, the Lord Jesus will clean that black finger. And He will do so thoroughly.

A pickpocket once said, "I have become a Christian. I used to nick about fifty, sixty watches per week, but I don't do so anymore. I only steal five or six."

Well, you see, that's not right. And now you are shaking your head, or maybe laughing about the pickpocket. But aren't you and I often just like him? No, we will not nick things, we won't steal, and we will not deceive. But avoiding a little bit of tax doesn't matter, does it, if you do it surreptitiously. That's acceptable, isn't it? Of course it isn't. None of that is acceptable. It is now possible to live a pure and holy life, because the Lord is with us wherever we go.

A sin that has not been confessed, no matter how small, a sin you have not repented of yet, is fully alive. We must realize that the Bible provides us with an answer to our sins. And that is wonderful. Often you think, especially when you regularly go to church, that you know what to do.

I will never forget a girl in Brazil who told me that she was losing her faith. She said, "At the time, I said yes to Jesus, and I thought that I had become a child of God, but I've got to be honest with you. I no longer believe in the Bible. I don't believe there is a God. Actually, I don't believe anything."

I read to her from the Bible that the Lord Jesus said that the Holy Spirit will convince us of sin, justice, and judgment. He will convince us of the sin of disbelief. It is a sin not to believe in Lord Jesus; it is an original sin, a great sin, a sin that leads to many other sins.

After a while, she said, "I now understand I have committed the sin of doubt."

I then said to her, "You know what you could do with that sin?"

"Certainly, I'll read my Bible."

"Will you please do that? It says in 1 John 1:9, 'If we confess our sins, he is faithful and just and will forgive us our sins and purify us from all unrighteousness.'"

She folded her hands and said, "Lord, please help me to stop doubting."

"But that is not asking for forgiveness; that isn't an answer to sin," I told her. "First you need to ask for His forgiveness, to be cleansed. And then you can ask the Lord to help you."

She understood. She humbled herself and said, "Lord, I have committed a great sin. I doubted You, everything the Bible teaches me, and what I used to believe. Will You forgive me?" When she spoke those words, she was forgiven.

I then said to her, "Now you can pray that other prayer too. First you need to confess and then trust that the Lord will place His strong hand on your weak hand. He will make you more than a conqueror; He will put you on victorious ground."

The words in 1 Peter 1:17–19 are quite serious: "Since you call on a Father who judges each man's work impartially, live your lives as strangers here in reverent fear. For you know that it was not with perishable things such as silver or gold that you were redeemed from the empty way of life handed down to you from your forefathers, but with the precious blood of Christ, a lamb without blemish or defect."

Really, holiness is a serious business. We are bought with the blood of Christ. We are bought at a very high price. Christians behave as if they belong to themselves, but don't forget that you lost all your rights at Golgotha. Every inch of us was paid for. Jesus paid the price. Have you given value for money?

Sometimes I give this example: Imagine, when I had a watchmaker's shop, you came to me and you bought a gold watch with a gold strap. Imagine that when I wrapped it up for you, I removed the gold strap and hid it. When you came home, you saw that you only had a watch. What would you do? You would say to everybody, "Don't ever buy something from Corrie ten Boom; she doesn't give you value for money."

If you and I do not give ourselves entirely to the Lord, we do not give Him the value He has paid for us on the cross. We were bought at a very high price. That cross was horrendous. It was an extremely high price to pay for you and me.

When I was a prisoner, I had an awful experience where I had to stand naked. I could hardly bear it. And then suddenly I remembered what was said about the Lord Jesus, that they divided His clothes among themselves. It was then that I understood a little more about the incredibly high price of that cross. That was because I was suffering the death on the cross in a small way. That was when I could say, "Oh Jesus, how could I compare my pain with Your physical pain, and Your emotional pain? Oh, Jesus, however much my soul suffers, one look at You strengthens my heart. Did You bear all that for me? For my incredible sin? Should I complain about my pain? And not suffer it with patience?"

Yes, it is a high price, but it has been paid. It is wonderful to be able to surrender to Him, who bought us. With body, soul, and spirit. And to lose your life for Him. It means you gain your life.

9

COMPLETE SURRENDER

I want to tell you what I learned about complete surrender. At one time surrendering was a great problem for me. Do you know the feeling? I simply didn't understand what it was and how to go about it. I then read a book by Andrew Murray, and it helped me greatly. It was a short book in which he wrote about a number of things, but there were a couple of chapters about complete surrender.

First I had to understand what it meant. So I read 1 Kings 20:1–4. Read it for yourself. Ben-Hadad, the king of Aram, took an army consisting of soldiers from as many as thirty-two allied countries and advanced to Samaria, the capital of Israel. Then he sent a message to King Ahab. And he said, "Your silver and gold are mine, and the best of your wives and children are mine" (1 Kings 20:3). Ahab answered, "I and all I have are yours" (1 Kings 20:4). Well, wasn't that complete surrender?

I have experienced surrender. When many years ago I was Adolf Hitler's prisoner, I had to surrender completely against my will. I was expected to obey. Ahab said to the conquering Ben-Hadad, "Just as you say, my lord the king. I and all I have are yours" (1 Kings 20:4). That was complete surrender.

And now we are dealing with somebody else. It is God, who is love. He isn't a dictator. He is a loving Father. There is no end to what He would like to do for us. There is no end to His blessings. Provided we surrender to Him.

I read a story about a little boy who was going to cross a long bridge with his father. A bridge without parapets. The little boy said, "Daddy, I am so frightened; just look at the high waves below us."

His father said, "Hold my hand, and nothing will happen to you." The boy laid his hand in his father's strong hand and his fear left him.

In the evening they had to return. Once again they had to cross that bridge on their own, but it was pitch black. "Daddy, I'm scared again. Can't you hear the water below us? It's so dark. You can hear those waves down there."

The father picked up his little boy in his arms and carried him to the other side, and the little boy fell asleep and didn't wake up until the next morning in his own bed.

You see, this surrender to God is quite different from Ahab's to Ben-Hadad. And from my surrender to Adolf Hitler. This is the kind of surrender God expects from us. And He gives you great peace.

As a child I used to enjoy singing, "Safe in Jesus' arms and safe in Jesus' heart." The Lord Jesus did not only die on the cross for your sins and mine, He is alive, and He said, "And surely I am with you always, to the very end of the age" (Matthew 28:20). Don't worry—lay your hand in His hand. You will be safe, even if life today feels like crossing a bridge without parapets over wild rushing water. Jesus is the Conqueror. Entrust yourself to Him.

10

IS SURRENDER NECESSARY?

Do we need to know what complete surrender means? Let's listen to what the Bible tells us about it. God expects us to surrender to Him. When we look at everything God has made, we might see what could help us to understand. The sun, the stars, the flowers, the trees — they are all in His power. We ourselves own objects, which we can only use when we hold them completely in our hands. The pen with which I am writing cannot be left partly in my pocket. Could God use you and me, if He had only part of us? God is life and love and blessing and power and endless beauty. And He is happy when He is united with His children who are prepared to be in Him. We are in Him and He is in us.

You will understand that I am now talking about those who know the Lord Jesus as their Savior and Lord. The first thing we need to do is what Jesus called being born again. If you know you are a sinner and ask Jesus to forgive your sins and to enter your heart, He will perform the miracle, which means you are born again. This is an important event. But we shouldn't forget that birth is a beginning. And now we must grow, which brings along the need for a renewed, complete surrender.

The absence of complete surrender on our side is an obstacle to God and prevents Him from blessing us and using us. He wants to make us a channel of flowing, living water. God can use us day and night if we surrender to Him completely.

Solomon's temple was *completely*—not just partly—dedicated to God. We all are a temple of the Holy Spirit, which is why we need to stop compromising, so that God can do blessed work through us. It is no longer what we can do, but what God can do. And often we experience that when we are weak, we are powerful, because we are relying on Him, on His power.

A woman in Russia, who was very ill, and who could hardly move, wrote books on an old typewriter. She could use only one finger, but with it she typed parts of the Bible, translations by Billy Graham, books by Watchman Nee, and even some writings by me. And she continued every day until she died. What was interesting was that the secret police never entered her room. They knew there was an old sick woman in there, whom they felt was of no interest to them. She was sheltered in the hiding place of the Highest of the Highest, and it was a strong castle. You see, if you belong to the Lord 100 percent, He will be accountable for you for 100 percent.

In my book *The Hiding Place*, I told the story of a dangerous battle during the last World War between the Germans and the Allies. It happened in the air, over Haarlem (near Amsterdam). It was the middle of the night and I was lying there, listening, and then I heard Betsie, my sister, in the kitchen. I thought, *I will go down too. Maybe we could have a cup of tea together. It's too noisy to sleep anyway.*

When I came back I saw a piece of shrapnel, the splinter of a grenade, lying on my pillow. I called Betsie and said, "If I hadn't joined you in the kitchen, I would be dead."

But she said, "There are no ifs when God is in charge."

That really comforted me. We are constantly under the Lord's supervision. That's why it is so peaceful. And that's why it feels so good to be with Him, day and night.

An electric train is always connected to electricity. A bus is different; it continually needs to fill with fuel. If we half-heartedly give ourselves to the Lord, for Him to use us, we are like buses. We constantly run out of fuel, and need fill-ups. We need to be like electric trains: continually connected to power. Then we will continue from strength to strength. To be connected to the Lord means that we are continually in His care.

Thank You, Lord Jesus, that You will be with us today and tonight and forever. Will You keep us from danger and protect us against fear? And will You show us the right way and not let go when we choose the wrong way and when we are in danger? It is wonderful to know that You take hold of our hands, that You hold us tight.

And when You hold us tight, You lead us on, all our life. And when You lead us on through life, there will be a day when You bring us home safely. Thank You, Lord Jesus. Amen.

11

ARE YOU AFRAID OF SURRENDER?

I would like to tell you what I have learned about complete surrender. Are you afraid of complete surrender? I would like to say a few things again about this subject: the surrender to our Savior, the Lord Jesus.

There was a time when I was afraid of it. "I can't really deal with it," I said. "You never know the consequences. I can't do it, nor do I know how I will manage. How will I be brave enough?" It is terrible to think in such a way about the Lord that we are afraid of consequences. I learned something which I will tell you now. To you who are afraid too, and don't know how to surrender.

You don't have to surrender on your own steam, or by your own willpower. God wants to work in us with regard to both willpower and completion. The start is what we call conversion, turning back to the Lord Jesus. It's as if you're living with your back turned to God. And you now need to turn 180 degrees towards Him. That is the wonderful first step. That is when Jesus makes you a child of God.

But now that child of God needs to grow. And once again, it means placing your weak hand in Jesus' strong hand, who wants to go with us and who wants to lead us. He is with us in our circumstances, our family, our worries, our work, our problems, even our suffering. We need to find the answer in serious prayer.

God, who is so powerful, and so full of love, wants to work in us to take away anything that is wrong, so that we surrender to Him what is wrong in our thoughts and actions. How did God use Abraham? God Himself turned him into a tool for His glory. And so you pray, "God, help me to be willing to be made willing."

I heard that prayer for the first time when I was in New Zealand. A theological student, Chris Lethbridge, had had an accident while swimming and had broken his neck. He was completely paralyzed from the neck down. He was very intelligent. He helped me correct a book which I had written in English. One evening, we talked about his terrible experience, and that no matter how terrible it was, he needed to surrender it. I told him that Betsie had said to me in a concentration camp, "We should not talk about our lives as they used to be, or what they may be like later when we are free. We need to be like prisoners, and surrender completely to the Lord. Then we will be able to accept."

At night I heard Chris pray, "Lord, make me willing to be made willing to surrender my life and everything, even my paralysis, to you." The next morning, his face shone with peace and joy.

If there's something you can't do and you don't dare to surrender, then pray that prayer: "Lord, make me willing to be made willing to surrender all." When you pray those words, our loving Savior will do so in you. Jesus led a life of complete surrender. He paid a high price for you. He lives in your heart with His Holy Spirit. You have hindered Him by your fear and your lack of willingness. He longs to help you. Trust Him by surrendering yourself to Him completely.

The Germans sing a song called "Casting Myself into an Ocean of Love." Yes, that is surrender to the Lord. There is no better way. No longer the ego-centered I, but the He. He in me, me in Him. When you throw an empty bottle in an ocean, it will immediately fill with and be surrounded by ocean water. If you throw yourself in Jesus' arms in complete surrender, you will be filled and surrounded by an ocean of God's love.

12

The Lord Helps Us Surrender

When it comes to surrender, it's not us who do it—it's the Lord.

It is the Lord who wants to help us surrender completely. The Holy Spirit tells us that we can submit ourselves to Him. But even if we do so, very often doubt arises in our hearts. "Did it really happen? Was the surrender complete?" you might ask yourself.

There is a wonderful text in the Bible which helped me greatly. A father came to Jesus for help for his son, who was possessed by a devil. "If you can do anything, take pity on us and help us," he pleaded with Jesus (Mark 9:21).

"If you can?" Jesus repeated. "Everything is possible for him who believes" (Mark 9:23).

The man cried out, "I do believe; help me overcome my unbelief!" (Mark 9:24).

We might say that this was an example of small faith. But meanwhile, it triumphed over the Devil! And the bad demon was cast out.

Go to the Lord and say, "Lord, I commit myself in complete surrender to you." Maybe you said it with a trembling heart; possibly you don't feel any strength, any certainty, but you will succeed. Don't be afraid; just come the way you are, and the power of the Holy Spirit will work in you.

I think of the Lord Jesus in Gethsemane. The Holy Spirit empowered Him to surrender completely, but still an incredible sense of despair, a fear, came over Him. If you happen to feel weakness and trembling, then simply trust God's Spirit working in you and surrender. And trust that God will accept you.

Just look at Him. Sometimes we are so occupied with ourselves, while we need to be occupied with God. Simply say, "Lord, I don't quite understand, but I will accept your conditions, and then I can and must surrender completely. Then you will bless me and turn me into a blessing."

When you say those words softly, and possibly with fear and trembling, but you still dare to speak them, be assured that God will take notice. He listens; He writes them in His book. And that is when He takes possession of you entirely. You might not feel it, you might not realize it, but you belong to Him completely.

Isn't it wonderful that we can discuss anything with Him? Anything! Do tell Him, tell Him anything. When you are in doubt, when you don't understand, no matter what you will still hear from Him. So don't only speak to Him, but listen to His voice.

The old story of the lost brooch really helped me. A lady lost a valuable brooch at the theater. She noticed it was missing when she arrived home. Early the next day she rang the caretaker of the theater and asked if he had found the brooch.

"No," he said, "but where was your seat? I will go and have a look if it is under your seat."

"My seat was on the fifth row, number two."

The man went to have a look and found the brooch. He went to the telephone and said, "Yes, I am pleased to tell you I found your brooch. Hello? Hello?"

There was no reply; she had impatiently hung up the phone. She will never know that her brooch was found.

The Holy Spirit teaches us to have great expectations for the Lord. Listen to the Lord. If you don't hear His voice immediately, wait patiently. Waiting for the Lord is a blessing too. He is a good Shepherd. And a good Shepherd speaks to His sheep. Don't put the receiver down too quickly. He loves you and has so much to say to you.

Lord Jesus, I thank You for loving us so deeply. Forgive us for being so restless at times and having so little patience to listen to You. Thank You that You are prepared to do all the things that we can't do. Please make clear to us everything about complete surrender, how to do it. Thank You for letting us know that when we surrender to You, You accept us. Hallelujah, what a Savior!

13

SURRENDERING TO THE FATHER

O nce again I'm going to talk about how a child of God should and may surrender to his heavenly father. It starts with being born as a child of God. The Lord Jesus calls it being "born again" (John 3:7). The Bible says, "So then, just as you received Christ Jesus as Lord, continue to live in him" (Colossians 2:6).

Somebody once said to me, "Several times I have surrendered to the Lord, in fact, only recently at a conference. And I felt so happy, but it only lasted a couple of weeks, and then I'd lost everything."

Well, if that is your experience, there needs to be a change in your direction of focus. You relied on yourself. And you couldn't manage by yourself. Now look up at Him, to whom you have surrendered. When God has started the job of your complete surrender, and when God has accepted your surrender, He will want to care for you and keep you. Do you believe it?

In this story of complete surrender, it is about two people: God and you. You are nothing; God is the eternal and almighty Lord. Are you afraid of entrusting yourself to that mighty Savior?

God is waiting for you. Don't you think that He can hold you, keep you day by day, minute by minute? Isn't it God who sees to it that the sun always shines, even though sometimes it may be behind the clouds? Don't you think that God can let His light shine on you and me, day by day, minute by minute, without a break? Why didn't you experience that? Because you haven't trusted Him.

A life of surrender might entail some difficulties. Not only is it difficult, it is impossible for us to keep it up. But by God's grace, by the power of the Holy Spirit who lives in us, that is exactly the life to which we have been called. Praise the Lord, He can and wants us to continue.

Have you ever heard of George Müeller? On his ninetieth birthday he was asked about the secret that made him happy and joyful at all times. He said, "There are two reasons. The first is that through God's grace I have always had a clear conscience, every day." The other one was that he loved God's Word, the Bible, so dearly. It is a beautiful description of a surrendered life: a clear conscience as a result of obedience to the Lord, every day, in His power and grace and in communion with the Lord; and by reading the Bible and praying.

First of all, you are prepared to do and work in the way God asks you to. On the other hand, you allow God to do what He wants to do. Surrender yourself to God's will. You don't always know what it is, but just say to yourself, "It is by Your grace, that I want to do Your will, in everything, every moment of every day." Just say, "Father God, I will not say one word without acknowledging Your glory. No activity without Your glory, everything according to Your blessed will."

Is that possible? What has God promised us? What the ear hasn't heard, what the eye hasn't seen, and what the human heart doesn't know—that is what God has prepared for those who love Him. You just can't imagine such blessings. They are divine riches.

I am now going to invite you to say something and to do something. Please say, "I surrender entirely to the Lord, to His will, to do only what He desires." God will enable you to work out your surrender. And now say, "I commit myself entirely to the Lord, so that He will work in me, so that I will live, according to His will and to please Him, as He has promised."

Yes, God wants to work in His children in a way we cannot comprehend. And He wants to do so every day, every moment. We need to give ourselves to Him in a childlike way. In complete trust.

14

Who Is Responsible for Our Surrender?

Who is responsible for our surrender? Let us talk and think again about the importance and beauty of the word *surrender.*

Ahab said to his enemy Ben-Hadad, "Just as you say, my lord the king. I and all I have are yours" (1 Kings 20:4). You see, when we say that to God, He blesses us. If you say that to Him, He will accept you and you will begin to learn what it means. To pour out tea, you take an empty cup. If you fill it first with ink or vinegar, you can't use the cup. God wants to fill us and bless us, when we have surrendered to Him completely, and when we have emptied ourselves.

A little while ago I was confronted by so many commitments that it almost frightened me. So many meetings, so much traveling, and more and more different kinds of work. I simply told the Lord about it. Isn't it wonderful that He understands you better than you understand yourself? And then the Lord asked me, "Have you given yourself to Me in complete surrender?"

I could reply, "Yes, Lord, for the full 100 percent."

"Then do you realize that you no longer have any possessions? You now are only the steward of what you possess. And that also means that you have no more responsibilities. They are Mine. You now need to follow Me obediently, and I will be your victory, your power, your everything."

I understood what God meant.

I remember being on my own in a prison cell. All I had were the clothes I was wearing. Life had been difficult before I entered the prison. We were responsible for hundreds of Jews who were in hiding, and many families. We provided food, took them to the hospital, arranged funerals, and hundreds of other responsibilities. When I arrived on my own in the cell there was a moment when I thought: *I've lost everything, I can't do anything, but I no longer have any responsibilities either.*

Other resistance workers had the same experience during the war. It would happen when they were alone in a cell after doing exciting and dangerous but often very successful work like rescuing children and adult Jews. And then suddenly they couldn't do anything. There was no safety, and they were there involuntarily. Just like Ahab, who was subjected to Ben-Hadad's power. But I now understood the concept: without possessions, and without responsibilities.

When the Lord asked me if I had surrendered everything to Him, it was quite different. It was a blessing, a complete wonderful surrender into His loving arms. And the fact that I now knew that not I, but He had complete responsibility, gave me such peace and rest. I suddenly saw how dynamic surrender to the Lord can be. His ability, His power, His complete understanding and perception, His love are far more than what I had considered to be my duty. In my short-sightedness, I thought I had to do everything with my own power, according to my abilities. But everything depends on *His* ability, *His* power.

Suddenly I saw Gideon, who was so weak and so scared. But the angel said to him, "The Lord is with you, mighty warrior" (Judges 6:12). Because the Lord was with him, he was a mighty warrior.

I was so delighted about this conversation with the Lord that I said, "Oh, Lord, I would love to see You."

"Look at your left hand," said the Lord.

And I saw that my hand was resting in another hand. And that hand was pierced. Jesus' pierced hand. I felt so safe. I was no longer alone, but He was in me. Jesus, crucified, but also the risen Lord. And glorified. He was in me; I was in Him.

It doesn't matter if we can't understand. It is impossible to understand, but it is so secure: hand in hand with Jesus. Quietly walking with Him. He is the Conqueror, and He wants to turn you and me into more than a conqueror, says the Bible. Hallelujah! What a Savior!

Thank You, Lord Jesus, that in Your great love, You want us to be completely Yours in order to fill us entirely with Your Holy Spirit. And by doing so, with Your love, Your joy, Your peace. Yes, Lord, listen to those who are praying together with me. You can see them,

Lord; they are listening to the radio. And you can hear them say together with me: "Take my life completely, I surrender to You, with wonderful, complete commitment." Hallelujah. Amen.

15

RELY ON THE LORD

In a large village in New Zealand I was meant to lead revival meetings during a full week. An active, believing Christian had invited me and prepared the meetings. She did this with such ability, so thoroughly, that the entire village was excited. Large banners had been strung across the streets with the words: "Corrie ten Boom is coming."

She belonged to the Baptists. This group of people didn't yet have a church building of their own, but they had purchased a big house with a large suite, which is where they held their church services. And she had now decided that she would furnish one of the rooms of the house as my bedroom, and would turn another room into a kitchen. "I will go there to cook for her each day and clean the house and look after her," she said.

Her doctor saw her one of those days and said, "You need to be careful and rest. You've taken too much on yourself."

"Right," she said. "I will rest when the week with Corrie ten Boom is over."

A few days before I arrived she had a heart attack and died. When I arrived, very little had been prepared. It was possible for me to sleep in the house and meals weren't a problem, but the people were rather desperate, as nobody knew what to do. The dear lady had wanted to do everything herself. Thankfully I didn't find it a problem, and the Lord did a lot at those meetings, and many people came to Him. Christians were encouraged to lead a happier and more active life in Him.

Thanks to her care, the program also included a day of rest on Thursday. I stayed in bed the whole day. But I tidied everything up, because I had understood that it wouldn't be a quiet day. And indeed it wasn't, because from early morning, throughout the entire day, people arrived for spiritual help. It was a wonderful, blessed day. I had plenty of time to talk to people.

Around five o'clock, I felt it had been enough. I heard another knock on the door, and I called out, "Do open the door, and then take the second door on your left." I called out again, because I realized that the footsteps had not progressed. "I'm not ill, do come in."

The door opened and there was a man in a boiler suit. He was a lorry driver. He looked at me with surprise in his eyes. "I saw a banner in the street. And I saw you were here. I had heard you speak a couple of weeks ago at a meeting far from here. I would have liked to have spoken to you at the time. Now I saw you were working in this village. I thought they will know in the Baptist Church where you are. And now I find you here myself. This is what I wanted to ask you: 'Why is Jesus a greater reality to you than to me?'"

I asked for wisdom, and I gave him this answer, "Because you have never surrendered to Him. If you do that now, He will reveal Himself to you as a very strong reality in your life."

The man knelt down and surrendered his life to Him, for whom he had longed so deeply.

During the week I was worried about the man whose wife had died that week. His grief was understandable. But I saw such despair in his eyes; it was too big. I prayed, "Lord, please send him to me, so that I can have a quiet chat with him. And please use me." Therefore I wasn't surprised when he knocked at the door one afternoon.

"Has my prayer been answered?" I said. "I would like to talk to you. Why are you so desperate? I can understand your grief, but your despair is too great, too strong. Don't give in to it."

He told me that spiritually he had relied entirely on his wife, that now he was alone he was out of his wits. We talked and prayed for a long time; we read the Bible. And he understood that he had to surrender his grief into the hands of the Lord, who wanted to make him independent and strong through His great love. He sees our trouble and grief, so that we can lay it in His hands, as is written in Psalm 10.

I told him about the strength with which he can submit everything. "We are fellow citizens of the kingdom of heaven, from where we expect the Lord to come, who will render our glorified body similar to His. He uses the same strength with which He helps us submit all things. That strength is enormous! More than enough to make you independent so that you can have communion with Him. And isn't it a wonderful future that you and your wife will meet again! Meanwhile there are great works waiting for you, through the Lord Jesus."

Later, I spoke to his son, who told me that his father had been used so wonderfully in the kingdom of God. Yes, God sees trouble and grief, which we can lay in His hands where it is safe, and where we are safe.

Thank You, Lord, that it is true. And thank You, that You also understand our suffering, our despair, our sadness so well. Because You, Lord Jesus, did not only bear our sins on the cross, but also our pain, which is why You understand us so well. Thank You for such great love. Amen.

16

GOD'S FOOLISHNESS

It is many years ago since I worked with the mentally disabled in Haarlem, a city west of Amsterdam. I ran several Bible clubs for them. It was a wonderful job.

You see, you and I need the Holy Spirit to understand and comprehend eternal truths. God's foolishness, which is the greatest wisdom, is one you can't understand with the wisdom of the wise. In 1 Corinthians 1 and 2 you can read a wonderful explanation. I always see two levels: the wisdom of the wise, which you receive by the grace of God; and a higher level, God's foolishness, which you can only understand through the Holy Spirit. Then you will see that that is the highest wisdom.

You should never try to bring down God's foolishness to the level of the wisdom of the wise, in order to try and understand it. It leads to ridiculous conclusions. Some then think that God is dead. They do so, because logical thinking becomes their guide. Mr. Anne van der Bijl once said, "What? God is dead? Of course not, I spoke to Him this morning." You see, in his quiet time he had experienced God's foolishness—that God who made heaven and earth, who had made him, this little human being, had spoken to him.

No, never belittle foolishness, God's highest wisdom, to judge it with the wisdom of the wise. If you want to see reality, you need to raise the wisdom of the wise to the level of God's foolishness. And then you will see and understand. The mentally disabled had very little wisdom of the wise. But the Holy Spirit gave them a lot of God's foolishness, which they accepted and understood without inhibition or doubt. It was then that I saw the importance of the words that we need to become like a child, because only then can we enter God's kingdom. Never could I tell them enough about God's love. Their faces would shine.

The father of one of the girls once asked me, "Why can't my daughter come to God's table? She loves the Lord. Does it matter that she has a learning disability?"

I said to him, "Pray about it for a week, and I will do the same." I did so, but I also went to a vicar with whom I talked about the possibility of her confirmation, if she could be baptized and come to God's table. I'm talking about fifty years ago. In those days these matters had not yet been considered. Nowadays it is much easier and much better. And the vicar and I prayed together, and he decided to include the mentally disabled. He said, "You will have to explain communion to the class; I can't do it in a simple way."

I then went to the class to interpret the official communion form. I talked about it as if it were a story. "Once upon a time there was a woman," I began to tell them, "who didn't believe that the Lord Jesus had died for her on the cross. She had never asked Him for forgiveness of her sins. And you know what she did? She took communion. She ate the bread and took the wine, which mean taking Jesus' body and blood, which will forgive us of our sins."

When they'd heard that story, the whole class said, "Oh, that's terrible!"

"Yes, isn't it, isn't it terrible, and you know who also said so? The Lord Jesus said so."

I never enjoyed taking communion so much as I did with this class. I knew that there was understanding, gratefulness, seriousness, which must have delighted the angels.

And the baptism, yes, Jake's the very tall guy. His intelligence was no greater than that of a six-year-old. He knelt down and heard those wonderful words spoken by the vicar: "Jake, I baptize you in the name of the Father and of the Son and of the Holy Spirit." He felt the water on his forehead, and Jake enjoyed it so much that he wanted to hold it in his hands. He didn't stand up, but he remained kneeling on the ground. I took his hand and led him back to his seat. But Jake kept his eyes closed. He didn't want to let go. How moving.

I will read a poem, which I happened to find somewhere:

*He had never had much intelligence; he was as naive
    as a child of four.
He only knew that his name was William, which
    pleased him to know.
His body grew old, but not his thinking, which
    remained childlike and immature.*

There was not much he could give to society, but in
*   church William was great.*
He would always sit close to the elders, because it
*   brought him near to the vicar.*
What he liked best about the service was the singing,
*   which in his way he was happy to join.*
His thoughts about God were simple; God was a
*   father, big, strong, and brave,*
Who was waiting for him in heaven, and Jesus
*   belonged to him, his big brother.*
He had never been able to read one single word, and
*   he'd never heard about a dogma.*
But he had never had any doubts, because he believed
*   every word his father said.*
When he fell seriously ill that Wednesday morning, he
*   immediately knew that it was his time to come.*
He had no fears, no worries, because Jesus would join
*   him on his journey.*
Although he had never understood what sin was,
*   although he had the simplicity of a child,*
God found in him such a great faith, one you will
*   seldom find in theologians.*

Thank You, Lord, for giving it to children, the mentally
disabled, and for giving it to us. And all that great-
ness we read about in the Bible which is for everybody,
including those who have listened just now. Thank
You, Lord Jesus, that You said, "Come to me, those
who are tired and burdened, and I will give you peace."
What a wonderful love, my Lord. Amen.

17

GOD'S MYSTERIES

In 1 Corinthians 4:1 – 2 Paul talks about Christ's servants who have been entrusted with God's mysteries. Such a guardian needs to prove to be reliable. Actually, it did not originally say servants or guardians, but stewards.

We first need to know what is meant by God's mysteries. What are they? Well, we can read about them in the Bible. God has revealed them to us. We understand a lot about the mysteries once we have opened our hearts to the Lord Jesus. He reveals them to us through His Spirit. And we should pass them on. I will mention one of them, John 3:16: "For God so loved the world that he gave his one and only Son, that whoever believes in him shall not perish but have eternal life."

If we are prepared to accept this amazing mystery of God, we need to pass it on. We need to be faithful and spread the news about this amazing truth and many other truths. It makes us so happy and thankful to know such a mystery. And what does God expect us to do? He expects us to be faithful, that is all. Love and obedience go together. But our task is not a small one. Paul talks about it: we are Christ's messengers, God's way of bidding us to be reconciled with Him.

Jesus said, "As the Father has sent me, I am sending you" (John 20:21). It means that each Christian should be a missionary. You in your small corner, and I in mine. Is it possible? Of course it is. Second Timothy 1:7 says, "For God did not give us a spirit of timidity, but a spirit of power, of love and of self-discipline." We need not rely on our own capabilities, but on God's. We need not depend on our limited strength, but on His unlimited power. Does this really mean that each Christian, whether called to be a housewife, a factory worker, or a tradesman, is in charge of God's mysteries? Are they stewards of His mysteries?

Three men were laying bricks. A passerby asked the first mason, "What are you doing?"

"I am building a wall," he replied.

The passerby asked the same question of the second mason. He replied, "I am earning a living to look after my wife and children."

But when the passerby asked the third mason what he was doing, he answered proudly, "I am building a cathedral."

My father had a watchmaker's shop. He would sometimes say to me, "My name is on the shop, while it's God's name that should be on it. I'm a watchmaker by the grace of God." Each Christian is building the kingdom of God, no matter whether you're a watchmaker, a mason, a housewife, or a professor, or wherever you may be called to be.

You can be quite original about your calling. A little while ago I was talking to a coal merchant. He told me he had two telephones beside each other. "Quite often I have two conversations using both phones," he said. "Down one I am giving spiritual care, and I talk about the Lord Jesus, while on the other one I'm taking an order for coal. It means they can both hear what I'm saying, I will ask the second one to wait a minute, and meanwhile he will be hearing the Word of God. When I have finished, I will ask, 'How much coal do you need?'" That is how he understood his calling to be a steward both of God's mysteries and simultaneously a steward of the coal business.

We are only asked to be faithful. Isn't it wonderful that we don't even need to try and be faithful relying on our own strength? In Galatians 5:22 we read about the fruit of the Spirit which also includes faithfulness. We will work together: He who commands us to be faithful on the one hand and us on the other. Paul says in 2 Timothy 2:13, "If we are faithless, he will remain faithful, for he cannot disown himself." Holding Jesus' hand, we remain faithful. And we can see our calling, even though everything may seem dark and lost.

My brother was imprisoned during the war. His father, his sisters, his son had been made prisoners too. He knew what might happen to prisoners in those days. He wrote the following poem.

> My dear young friends, we were born in a time of
>   trouble and strife.
> Events will destroy everything, the Devil's actions,
>   causing me to suffer.

But I don't want to mope away my days, nor lose
*   myself in a delusion of sin.*
A terrible time? No, a wonderful time, because Christ
*   the Lord is fighting for His young people.*
My dear young friends, we were born in a world
*   which has been promised total peace.*
And where God's Son, destined for eternity, laid the
*   foundation for reconciliation Himself.*
And whoever has not yet surrendered to Him, I know
*   He is the way, the truth, and the life.*
A terrible time? No, a wonderful time, because Christ
*   the Lord is fighting for His young people.*
My dear young friends, we were born for a future in
*   which we will be able to spread our wings again.*
The battle with Satan was lost a long time ago, when
*   he was vanquished by the cross.*
The King's case is still winning; God wants me to
*   cooperate and begin today.*
A terrible time? No, a wonderful time, because Christ
*   the Lord is fighting for His young people.*

Christ the Lord is fighting for His young people. Whoever believes in me, says the Lord, in the works I do, will do them too, and they will be greater than Mine, because I am going to the Father. How is that possible? To perform greater things than Jesus did? You? Me? Yes, because Jesus is at the right hand of God the Father, and He will do great things, greater than He did in His three and a half years in Palestine, but He's doing it through His followers. You and me. And that is how He turns us into His stewards, guardians of God's mysteries.

Thank You, Lord Jesus, for giving us such wonderful work to do. Thank You for using us and because You, Lord Jesus, fight beside Your young people. Thank You for always giving us faithfulness, love, strength, and courage through Your Holy Spirit. Hallelujah, Amen.

18

GOD'S TREASURES

The Lord Jesus has given us a task. Jesus said, "Go into all the world and preach the good news to all creation" (Mark 16:15). This is the gospel, which contains all our Lord's treasures. And we need to share those treasures with others.

We all need to go where God sends us. Each Christian has a calling: you have yours, and I have mine. There is a world that needs saving. Do you love the Lord Jesus? Love and obedience go together. You have a task. Complete it. Can't you? I can't either. We don't have enough strength and resources in ourselves to share with others, but our Lord has many treasures, very many treasures. That is why we need to study our bank account, the Bible.

All God's promises are in Jesus, yes, amen. There are many we need to share with, and that's why we need many of God's treasures. "Finally, be strong in the Lord and in his mighty power" (Ephesians 6:10). No branch can bear fruit by itself; it must remain in the vine. Neither can you

bear fruit unless you remain in Jesus. It is how you and I
need to remain connected with the source of our strengths,
Jesus, our vine.

I hope that you Christians who are listening can clearly
see the task and treasures you have been given, now that you
are a child of God. But you who are listening, and know
that you are not a Christian, this message is for you too. In
the eyes of the Lord, your life is like a wilderness. But you
can become God's garden. What should you do; what could
you do? Accept Jesus. In John 1:12 we read: "Yet to all who
received him, to those who believed in his name, he gave
the right to become children of God." But it means you also
have a job to do, a task.

You can read about many of our Lord's treasures in the
Bible. Would you like to attend a crash course? All you need
to do is listen to the Master when He teaches a large group
of followers, whom He sent out into the world to become
the light. He described all kinds of treasures, which were
there for them, and you can read about them in Matthew 5,
6, and 7: the Sermon on the Mount. But it's not just a matter of listening: "Therefore everyone who hears these words
of mine and puts them into practice is like a wise man who
built his house on the rock" (Matthew 7:24).

But your crash course, the Sermon on the Mount, is very
short. There is a complete manual, which we need to study
time and time again, which is the Bible. You may say, "But
I don't understand it." No, we can't understand it, not by
ourselves. But the Lord Jesus promised us in Acts 1:8, "You
will receive power when the Holy Spirit comes on you." And
the Holy Spirit will give you understanding, strength, and

faith. He explains all the Lord's different treasures and all you need to be a happy, victorious child of God. Yes, you will then experience what is said in Acts 1:8: "You will be my witnesses in Jerusalem, and in all Judea and Samaria, and to the ends of the earth."

Paul says in Ephesians 1:3, "Praise be to the God and Father of our Lord Jesus Christ, who has blessed us in the heavenly realms with every spiritual blessing in Christ." They are the amazing treasures. After all, He has chosen us in Him before the foundation of the world, so that we can be holy and pure as we stand before Him. In love He picked us, destined us to be accepted by Jesus Christ, as His sons, to satisfy His will, to praise the wonder of His grace with which He blessed us in His love. We are saved in Him, by His blood, the forgiveness of our trespasses, according to the wealth of His grace.

Just read on what it says. What an inventory! Yes, Jesus is our peace. Just ask the Lord to help you see through His Holy Spirit, reading the Bible, what amazing treasures of your Lord you can share with the poor world around you.

Thank You, Lord Jesus, that through reading the Bible all Your treasures are continually laid in our hands. Use us today to share them with others. Make us real children of light. Give us a wonderful and continuous experience of the joy of sharing Your treasures. Hallelujah! Amen.

19

Ask Anything

Today I will be talking to those who've really said yes to the Lord Jesus. Mind you, the message is for anybody, but especially for those who have committed themselves.

He came into your life and into your heart. And did you know how important that is? Because you are worth so much in God's eyes, the angels rejoiced in your response. The Bible speaks of the dark coming into the light. And indeed the Lord Jesus gives us peace, a peace that passes all understanding. The Lord compares it to conversion, being born again. You can read about it in the discussion with Nicodemus in John 3.

Yes, the word *conversion* is a very clear and good word. It means a 180-degree conversion. At first we live turned away from God, even when we live a decent life. When you accepted the Lord Jesus, you turned around. Now you are living toward God. But you're still like a baby. A born-again baby. It's a start. A baby needs food and care and love. And it is all there in that wonderful book called the Bible.

Sometimes I call the Bible a checkbook. Yes, honestly, all the promises in the Bible are now for you, checks written in your name, and signed by Jesus. For instance, read Romans 5:5: "God has poured out his love into our hearts by the Holy Spirit, whom he has given us," then say, "Thank You, Lord, that is for me." It is as if you have endorsed the check by writing your signature on the back. In this way the Bible becomes a love letter from God, your heavenly Father. And now, you will not live like the poor; you will live a rich life. C. S. Lewis once wrote: "Too many Christians are like children who are happy playing in a puddle in their back garden, while they have been invited to spend a day on the beach."

When you became God's child by responding positively to the Lord Jesus, the Lord opened His treasury of heavenly riches. And He invited you to enter and to take everything freely. Yes, right now you are infinitely rich, as long as you do not limit yourself by lack of faith. Well, that's exactly what troubles me, you might say. My faith is so small and so weak. I am so happy that in Hebrews 12:2 it doesn't say, "Let's rely on our faith," but "Let us fix our eyes on Jesus, the author and perfecter of our faith."

When I had a watchmaker's shop, before the war, there might be a new watch in my shop that didn't keep accurate time. I never tried to repair it, but sent it straight back to the manufacturer. And when he had repaired the watch, it would always come back to me running accurately.

When my faith doesn't run smoothly, I never try to repair it, but I send it back to Jesus, the manufacturer, the author and perfecter of my faith. And when He repairs it, it works so precisely.

We don't need a great faith, but we need faith in a great God. So often we look at our faith, and it can discourage us so much. In New Zealand we sometimes went to remote missionary posts by car; often we crossed very primitive bridges. The driver would first investigate the bridge to see if it was strong enough to carry the car. And when he was sure, he would drive across. And if you were to ask me now, "What carried the car, our trust in the bridge, or the bridge itself?" we immediately would know the answer: it was the bridge.

Sometimes people say, "Corrie, it was your faith that carried you through your time in the concentration camp during the war." And I will immediately answer, "No, it wasn't my faith; it was the Lord who did it. He was the One who made my faith strong by His Holy Spirit, who makes faith work in our hearts. He's the One who does it. He did it. Hallelujah!"

Do you know what the Holy Spirit teaches us? How to pray. You can really tell the Lord anything you like.

I once spoke to somebody one day after she had accepted the Lord Jesus as her Savior. And she said to me, "It's so wonderful to know that I will never be alone again, but I can tell Him anything."

The wonderful thing about praying is that you leave a world of not being able to do something, and enter God's realm where everything is possible. He specializes in the impossible. Nothing is too great for His almighty power. Nothing is too small for His love.

It became clear to me when I was in the difficult class of God's school, in a prison, during the last World War, after my family, friends, and I had saved Jews and had been imprisoned in concentration camps. I had been in the concentration camp a couple of weeks when I said to Betsie, my sister, "What should I do? I have a cold, I don't have a handkerchief."

"Pray," she said, and I laughed. But she folded her hands and prayed, "Father, in Jesus' name, I pray to You, please will You give Corrie a handkerchief? She has a cold. Amen."

Yes, I laughed again, but do you know what happened? I heard someone call my name. I went to the window where I saw a friend of mine, a fellow prisoner, who worked in the hospital.

"Here," she said, "take this, a little gift for you."

I opened the parcel and it was a handkerchief. "Why on earth are you giving me a handkerchief?" I asked. "Did you know I had a cold?"

"No, but I had found an old sheet, and I made a couple of handkerchiefs out of it, and then there was a voice in my heart which said: 'Take a handkerchief to Corrie ten Boom.'"

Can you imagine what a handkerchief means to you at that moment? That handkerchief told me that there is a God in heaven who hears when one of His children is praying on a small planet, the earth, for something incredibly small. And that God in heaven tells one of His other children to give Corrie ten Boom a handkerchief.

Yes, that is God's foolishness. He is wiser than the greatest wisdom of man. You can read what Paul says about this in 1 Corinthians 1 and 2. He speaks very clearly about the wisdom of the wise, and the foolishness of God.

Just imagine a little child crying because an old doll has broken. She takes it to her father. Would her daddy say, "My dear child, throw it away; that old doll isn't worth a penny." No, on the contrary, he will say, "Come here, my child. Daddy will try to repair the doll."

Why on earth would such a big man take such a silly old doll seriously? Because he sees it through the eyes of the little one. And because he loves his little one. And in the same way God sees your problems through your eyes because He loves you. And nothing, nothing is too small for His love. Just tell Him anything.

Thank You, Father, in Jesus' name, that we can tell You anything. You listen to us and You answer our prayers, because You love us dearly. Thank You that You Yourself teach us how to pray and how to believe through Your Holy Spirit. Hallelujah, what a Savior! Amen.

20

ANGELS:
MINISTERING SPIRITS

A ngels are ministering spirits.
We read and hear so much about demons today. Many books were published last year, and it's so good to read that demons are defeated enemies, but in the meantime they can still rant and rave and cause people considerable trouble. They are servants of darkness. It is good for us to be aware of the danger. Many people are unaware of the fact that spiritism, astrology, and fortune-telling are all occult practices and the work of demons.

It is also good to know that we are victorious through the blood of the Lamb and the words of our testimony. The Lord Jesus taught us that we can and must cast out demons in His name. Our battle against the powers of evil is a victorious battle, and those who are with us are far greater than those who are against us. We have a great High Priest and legions of angels on our side.

Recently I have been studying the Bible to see what it says about angels, and it is wonderful that there's much more in the Bible on the subject than I had ever imagined — wonderful because angels are ministering spirits sent to help those who will inherit salvation. Hebrews 1:14 tells us that. We are dealing with angels constantly, even though we're not always aware of them.

Are there angels here on earth? What do they look like? Do they have any influence on the history of mankind? Do they really have anything to do with the lives of human beings? The Bible writers believed in them and thought they were important because they wrote about them hundreds of times, much more than about evil spirits and Satan. So why do we hear so little about them these days?

What great value to know how strong our position is in the great final battle before Jesus' second coming. Undoubtedly, angels have much work to do on earth at this time of terrible attacks by the Evil One. When you read the paper it seems as if the world is full of sin and disasters, air pollution, hijacking, and murder. What a world! Who is it who will conquer this world? He who believes that Jesus is the Son of God. John tells us that, and that means that you and I, who believe in Him, stand on the frontline of an enormous battle, not against flesh and blood but against the representatives of the Devil's headquarters. Let's see which allied forces are on our side.

Satan sometimes appears as an angel of light, so we have to be able to discern well. Of course, his soldiers, the demons, will certainly be trying to do that too. In fact, the Lord Jesus spoke of what will happen before His second coming, saying that if it were possible, even the elect could be deceived (Mark 13:22). Fortunately it says "if" it were possible, which means it is not possible. We need discernment of spirits, and the Holy Spirit wants to give us that.

In his book *The Screwtape Letters*, C. S. Lewis warns of two dangers. The uncle devil writes to his nephew, who works on earth, "Ensure that people do not believe that we exist, that's the first thing. But if people do know we exist, work in such a way that they have an unhealthy interest in us and think and talk about us a lot."

Now, we see that happening a lot these days, so we are going to do exactly the opposite in a couple of these radio messages. We are going to speak about angels! And that is a much happier study than finding out what evil spirits are and what they do. God is still a God of miracles, and in the future, when we can expect much worse things, He will save and rescue us in many unusual ways. We will experience the fact that the need is not greater than the Helper.

Horace DuBose wrote: "I expect that in the last days before the great re-creation of the world, a renewed demonstration will come from angels to those who will inherit salvation. In the past angels have achieved a great deal for mankind and the nations. The Bible speaks of their work on earth three hundred times. We can therefore learn a lot about them in the Bible, what they did and were, in the days which the Bible describes, but we should also realize what angels are doing now and in the future. Their presence and actions help change defeat into victory."

Lord, will You please protect us from the Enemy as we speak, listen, and read the Bible about Your blessed angels. Will You grant us wisdom and lead us in this study by Your Holy Spirit? We thank You, Lord, that we know Your angels are there and may—and must—help us. In Jesus' name, amen.

21

ANGELS:
WHAT KIND OF BEINGS?

Are angels a reality? Do they have a shape? Are they visible? What is their task? What is their relationship to mankind, to this world? Can intelligent people really believe that they exist? Heathen philosophers, such as, among others, Socrates and Plato, speak of good spiritual beings, but we should preferably keep to what God says in His Word.

Let us look in the Bible for the answers. In the letter to the Hebrews we read a lot about what angels are *not*. Read it for yourself, especially in the first chapter. In Colossians 1:16 Paul writes that angels were created by God, by Him and for Him. Angels have their own language; read 1 Corinthians 13. Jude, verse 6, writes of a place where they live.

When I read of what the angels did in the time that the Bible was written, they were real pacesetters. "Hurry up!" is their word. "Get up and go!" Peter, Gideon, Joseph, Philip—it was always the same. When the baby Jesus was in danger, they said to Joseph, "Go to Egypt as soon as possible — hurry up!"

When people saw angels, they looked like young men, never like beautiful women and never with wings. Cherubs have wings, but they are actually different heavenly creatures than the angels. Perhaps they are visible, but our eyes cannot see them because there are light waves which we cannot distinguish. People can only see angels if the Lord performs a miracle, if He considers it necessary. Sometimes animals can distinguish them better. Balaam's donkey saw the angel before his master saw him.

I had a wonderful experience in South Africa. The program was much too full, but the work was going extremely well. But one day I had five meetings and I was so glad to leave for home at 9:30 p.m. Then they told me that I still had a sixth meeting to go, but I refused. Their disappointment was so great that I understood that I had to go. "It's a very important party at a prestigious club," they told me. "They have advertised widely saying that you will be speaking. There are souls to be won; many of the guests have never heard the gospel."

So I went, but I felt absolutely exhausted. When I started to speak, I suddenly felt my strength returning. The Lord gave me a powerful, joyful message.

Afterwards a young man came up to me and asked, "Was it difficult to speak to us?"

"Why?" I asked.

"The whole time you were speaking, I saw a large angel standing behind you. He held his hand above your head as if he were protecting you."

I asked a friend who was there, "Did you see anything while I was speaking?"

"Yes, there was a light behind you all the time you were speaking."

And someone else said, "You looked so tired, but suddenly all the weariness was gone and you spoke so powerfully."

That was a lovely experience.

Angels have superhuman power. They are immune to heat and fire. Samson's father, Manoah, saw an angel coming out of the fire from the altar (Judges 13:19–20). Nebuchadnezzar saw an angel with Shadrach, Meshach, and Abednego, who had been cast into the fiery furnace (Daniel 3:24–25). All four were completely unharmed by the flames. Peter writes that they were great in power and strength.

David describes angels in Psalm 103:20 as obedient servants, but there were some who remained with Lucifer (Satan, the Devil) when he rebelled against God, and they were judged with him. So angels had a choice between good and evil.

Angels don't know everything. For example, the Bible says that they do not know the day or the hour of Jesus' second coming.

I spoke recently in a church where they were making a television recording. There was an irritating light that shone brightly on my face. I prayed, "Lord, I don't know whether there are angels here, but if so, please place an angel between me and the light so that I won't be distracted by it." From that moment on, the light was no longer bright. When I saw the videotape later, the recording was good from start to finish.

I believe that we may ask for the help of angels. We may enjoy their assistance and thank God for them, but we may only worship Him who is worthy, the King of Kings, the Lord Jesus Christ before whom every knee will bow. The Lamb who was slain and who is worthy to receive all honor, splendor, power, and worship. Many angels, thousands, yes, numerous angels will worship Him, our Savior and Lord, together with us. A wonderful future!

Thank You, Lord, that You sent us so many angels as our assistants and guardians and that they help us so much more than we realize. Most of all, we thank You for being with us, always, until the end of the world. Hallelujah! Thank You, Lord Jesus. Amen.

22

ANGELS: THEIR WORK

Angels have a gift and an assignment to praise and thank the Lord, often through their music and song. They were present at the creation of the earth. In the book of Job you can read about their discipline and assignment for which they had to report regularly for duty. In Job 38:7 mention is made of a choir of angels that was present at the creation. Their singing in the fields of Bethlehem is most well known, when one angel brought the message and a multitude sang the chorus, "Glory to God in the highest, and on earth peace to men on whom his favor rests" (Luke 2:14).

Angels are not omniscient, but they do know more than we do. In the Bible it says that we are a little less than the angels. In another place it says that we are a little more than them. It is clear that they are interested in and sympathize with us people when the Lord Jesus says that there is joy amongst the angels about every sinner who repents, and I am sure that their singing puts their joy into words.

There are different ranks among the heavenly beings. We do not know how many. The Bible speaks of two important classes: the cherubim and the seraphs. When Adam and Eve were banished from the Garden of Eden, cherubim stood at the east side to prevent them from coming back. Hezekiah, a man who knew a great deal about God and eternal matters, lived, if I may say so, in a childlike manner with the Lord. Taking the ugly letter he received from Sennacherib, King of Assyria, during the siege of Jerusalem, he spread it out before the face of the Lord at the temple. Then he prayed a powerful prayer, beginning with these words, "O Lord, God of Israel, enthroned between the cherubim, you alone are God over all the kingdoms of the earth" (2 Kings 19:15).

In Ezekiel 10 we read of cherubims, wheels, and wings. It was a wonderful event in the temple, where the cherubim glorified the Lord God with loud voices. It was an incomprehensible event; the cherubim were described as strange beings, but then suddenly in verse 21, "under their wings was what looked like the hands of a man."

The angels who work on earth are frequently described in the Bible as friendly, understanding helpers. Read about Peter's liberation in Acts 12:1 – 11. The murder of James was so appreciated by the Jews, that the king decided to kill Peter too. He was taken to the prison, guarded by a considerable number of soldiers. He was to be tried after the Passover. Peter slept with his hands chained to the hands of two soldiers. There were sentries at the doors and in the corridors. Then an angel of the Lord appeared in the cell and light shone immediately. It seems that all the sentries were asleep. Read how and what the angel did.

First he shook Peter awake and had him stand up. "Stand up, quickly!" he said. The chains fell off Peter's wrists. "Put on your clothes and sandals," he ordered, and then, "Wrap your cloak around you and follow me." It is so wonderful to read how the angel arranged things in the smallest details. At first Peter could not believe that it was really happening; he thought that it was a vision. The angel went ahead of him through opened doors and walked through the gate with Peter and took him a little way into the street. Then he disappeared, and Peter only believed it was real once he was standing alone in the street at night.

The angels are no less active today than they were in biblical times. Missionaries in the Congo told me of an experience they once had. In a home, a kind of boarding school, were two hundred missionary children. The Mau Maus decided to kill all the children and their teachers. From the home, they saw a large group of Mau Maus approaching, so they all knelt down and prayed for protection. There was only a small hedge around the home and a few soldiers lived with them, but that meant nothing against the superior strength of the enemy. Suddenly they saw the rebels turn around and run away. The same thing happened the next day, and again on the third day. Then they stayed away.

One of the rebels was wounded, and was taken to the mission hospital by people who had found him on the side of the road. When the doctor was bandaging his wounds, he asked, "Why didn't you come into our house? You'd planned to kill us, hadn't you?"

The man answered, "We couldn't. We saw hundreds of soldiers in white uniforms and we were scared to death."

In Africa soldiers never wear white uniforms. Those people had seen angels. The missionaries understood that it was angels. What a great God and a loving Father we have, that He sent these ministering spirits to protect those who will inherit salvation.

Thank You, Father in heaven, that we know angels are here. Your angels were not only active in biblical times, but they also surround us now. Thank You for Your great love which is the reason behind this. In Jesus' name. Amen.

23

ANGELS: MESSENGERS

In Hebrews 1:14 we read of angels being sent out to minister to those who will inherit salvation. Yes, a messenger service, that is what they had, throughout the centuries that they were described in the Bible. An angel had to take the message to Lot that Sodom and Gomorrah would be destroyed (Genesis 19:12–13).

In the book of Daniel we read a lot about their messenger service. What a warning the angel had for Belshazzar, king of the Chaldeans, who at the heathen banquet was enjoying his binge with a thousand party guests. The angel wrote on the wall, "Mene, mene, tekel, parsin ... You have been weighed on the scales and found wanting" (Daniel 5:25, 27). The king saw only the hand of the angel writing this on the wall. That night the king was slain, together with his drunken party guests.

And there is this beautiful story. Daniel was praying. He confessed his sins and the sin of his people Israel. Then Gabriel came and said, "Daniel, I have now come to give you insight and understanding." And then Daniel received some of the most detailed and amazing prophesies of the whole Bible. Read about it in Daniel 9.

When Jesus came to earth, in the fullness of time, the angels were very busy with their messenger service. First Zechariah and then Mary and later on, Joseph on several occasions. The angels had many messages to deliver. And then, the most glorious telegram: "Today in the town of David a Savior has been born to you; he is Christ the Lord" (Luke 2:11).

What a link these blessed angels make between heaven and earth! What can we expect from them? What can you expect from them? I do not know. But this I certainly believe, when a child of God passes away, an angel receives the command to accompany you and me. Poor Lazarus was carried to heaven by the angels. Just imagine how glorious that will be. But we need their help now, and you can count on it that they are here now.

As a child I sang a song:

When I go to sleep at night, fourteen angels follow me.
Two on my right side, two on the left,
Two at the head of the bed, two at the foot,
Two to cover me, two to wake me,
Two to show me the way to heavenly paradise.

That is not biblical, you will say. I know that. But I think we expect too little, rather than too much. Billy Graham writes that he is sure that angels protect him on all his journeys. I have always expected that myself, and if I am in a plane I always thank the Lord for the angels that surround us, who help the pilots whenever necessary.

Some of you who are listening may think, "But wait a minute, can I enjoy that now? Can I be sure of it?" In Hebrews 1:14 it says, "Are not all angels ministering spirits sent to serve those who will inherit salvation?" Is that for me? That is a very good question. The Father's house with many rooms is for the children of God. Are you not a child of God? Or are you not sure that you are? Then something definitely needs to happen, something wonderful.

To those who accept Him, Jesus gives the power and right to become children of God. Jesus says, "Come to me, all you who are weary and burdened, and I will give you rest" (Matthew 11:28). Come to Jesus. Accept all the blessings He wants to give you. Salvation, cleansing from sin, forgiveness, rest. Tell it all. He understands you better than people do, better even than your friends understand you. Say it in your own words. Something like, "Lord Jesus, I am not sure whether I belong to You. I believe that You died on the cross for the sins of the whole world. I have sinned too. I know only too well that I am a sinner. Will You forgive me? And cleanse my heart? And make me strong, with You, to win the battle against sin?"

Then it is good to set your house in order and tell Him about the sins you are aware of. David taught us that we can even pray, "Forgive my hidden faults" (Psalm 19:12). When you do this for the first time, the Lord Jesus calls this being "born again" (John 3:3). That is a beginning. He wants to remain with you and show you the way to go.

When I was confirmed in church years ago, my text was, "Whoever claims to live in him must walk as Jesus did" (1 John 2:6). He wants to hold you tight and walk with you. And if Jesus holds your hand, then He will hold you tight. And if He holds you, He will lead you on. And if He leads you on, then He will bring you safely home. And that is inheriting salvation. And then there is already here the wonderful presence of angels who want to help you.

Lord Jesus, thank You that You will absolutely never throw out or turn away those who come to You. Thank You, that all may come, including those listening to the radio who have said their "Yes" to You. Maybe very quietly, but You heard it. Thank You that the angels are now their helpers and protectors. Hallelujah! What a Savior!

24

INTERCESSION

Work to be done! Intercession.

Isn't it wonderful that we are called to be intercessors? And anybody can be one. Do you realize that not one of your intercessory prayers will be lost? Not one! Sometimes we forget. The Devil may laugh at our plans. He smiles when we are up to our eyes in work. But he quakes when we pray. When we are faithful intercessors he often says to us, "Shouldn't you stop? You have been doing this for such a long time, and can't you see, the Lord doesn't listen." But he is a liar. Not one of our prayers is lost.

I experienced it so wonderfully a little while ago. When I was five I asked the Lord Jesus to come into my heart and immediately the Lord turned me into an intercessor. My mother told me later that I always concluded each of my prayers with the words, "And Lord, please convert all the people in Smedestraat." Smedestraat was a street behind our house, and there were several pubs, and you would always see people drunk, which really concerned me. Just imagine, a small child of only five praying for an entire street. But God heard me.

A while back I was invited to be interviewed by Dutch presenter Willem Duys. He was somebody who spoke on television and he asked me several questions. It was an opportunity to bring the gospel, to really witness. Afterwards, I received a lot of letters. And one of those letters was written by a lady who said, "My husband was delighted to hear you were from Haarlem. He also lived in Haarlem. He had always lived in Smedestraat. And when you talked and witnessed he said, 'This is wonderful because we can now write to her and tell her that I too love the Lord Jesus.'"

To me this was a wonderful reply. It was about seventy years after I, a little girl of five, had prayed for people in Smedestraat, and now one of them brought me this message that he knew the Lord. When we enter heaven we will be surprised to see that those we prayed for have been saved for eternity, through our intercessions.

I remember praying for a fellow student at my domestic science school when I was a fifteen-year-old girl. I had always attended a Christian school and now I was attending a non-faith school, and oh, how concerned I was for my fellow students and for the teachers. When I came home I would often say, "Mother, please pray with me for them, because they won't accept the Lord immediately."

My mother said, "Well, my child, you will discover that life is not like a Christian school. You will find out that people do not come to the Lord straightaway."

After I had been interviewed by Willem Duys, I received a letter from a lady who wrote, "It was wonderful seeing you on television. You and I went to the same school, to the domestic science school in Sneevochtstraat in Haarlem. And now sixty years later, I suddenly see you on television."

Well, that was so special that I went to visit her the following day. And I could bring her the gospel. Can you see that this was a miracle? Sixty years ago I had prayed for my fellow students, and now sixty years later, I could bring one of them to the Lord. You know, the mills of God grind slowly, yet they grind exceedingly small.

Do you find it difficult to intercede? It says in one of the hymns: "Nothing can be wrested from God, not by complaining or through pain, He wants us to pray to Him." Even if you find it very difficult, you shouldn't give up, because Romans 8:26–27 gives us this wonderful consolation where it says, "We do not know what we ought to pray for, but the Spirit himself intercedes for us with groans that words cannot express. And he who searches our hearts knows the mind of the Spirit, because the Spirit intercedes for the saints in accordance with God's will."

Isn't it amazing? The Holy Spirit prays together with you and me, and that is why our prayers are always heard. Hallelujah!

Oh, Lord, how wonderful that You hear our intercessions. You know, Lord, that some of us prayed such a long time ago for our daughters, for our sons, for our mothers, fathers, brothers, husbands, and wives, for anybody in need. And so often that thought crept in, maybe I had better stop. But I thank You, Lord, that no intercessions are lost. And thank You, Holy Spirit, that You teach us how to intercede, and together we will win, You and I. Hallelujah! Amen.

25

PRAY FOR EACH OTHER

When Paul writes about the armor of God, which we need for us to be strong in the Lord, and to be enveloped in the power of His might, he says in Ephesians 6:18–20, "And pray in the Spirit on all occasions with all kinds of prayers and requests. With this in mind, be alert and always keep on praying for all the saints. Pray also for me, that whenever I open my mouth, words may be given me so that I will fearlessly make known the mystery of the gospel, for which I am an ambassador in chains. Pray that I may declare it fearlessly, as I should."

There are many missionaries who need these prayers at the moment. A missionary once was in great danger. One evening, he was alone at home, and enemies wanted to kill him. But nothing happened.

The next day one of those enemies came to him and said, "We wanted to kill you last night, but we couldn't."

"Why couldn't you?"

"There were so many men around your house, and there were only four of us, and around your house there were at least seventeen men."

The missionary wrote about this to his friends in his home country and they worked out that they had had a prayer time that very evening. Seventeen Christians had come to pray. Seventeen Christians had prayed in his native country, and seventeen angels stood in front of the missionary's house.

Satan laughs when we try hard. He mocks our wisdom, but he trembles when we pray.

You see, when you pray for somebody, it is as if you are standing next to the Lord. You discuss the needs of your fellow men with each other. Some say you need to show "solidarity." But I think you must be careful. I don't think it is right to try and identify with someone who is sinking in despair or sin. It could break you; it can be infectious, and most of all, it is not necessary. Jesus bore all pain and sin on the cross, and it was completed.

Can anybody in the whole world understand pain as well as Him who bore it on the cross? Can anybody understand despair and the danger of sin better than Him, He who paid for it with His blood? Who did it with such great love, an ocean of divine love? That's why, together with Him, we can understand pain and sin and see them in their true light. He bore the punishment, which brings us peace. His lashes have healed us.

Therefore interceding for somebody is not a case of repairing somebody's soul; instead the soul breaks through and makes contact with God. The soul is renewed. We can only truly intercede when we pray based on the reality of God's salvation in Jesus Christ. As an intercessor in God's kingdom, you need to keep in step with God and what He's telling you about reality, otherwise you will be trampled upon. When you know too much, more than God wants you to know, you will be so oppressed by the situation that you cannot break through to reality.

Intercession is so incredibly important. A little girl prayed for her friend until she, like her friend, accepted the Lord Jesus as her Savior. Then the two of them began to pray for a third girl, and then the three of them for a fourth girl, and the four of them for a fifth friend. This was a chain reaction in the hearts of small children through intercession.

Will you ask the Lord to use you for that chain reaction and that He may begin in your heart and then continue? First pray for one, then pray with both of you for a third person, and then with the three of you pray for a fourth person. Paul says in 1 Timothy 2:1, "I urge, then, first of all, that requests, prayers, intercession and thanksgiving be made for everyone."

I have noticed that nothing is as liberating as interceding for others. What a task, but simultaneously what a delightful job.

Lord Jesus, will You turn us into good intercessors? We can tackle anything together with You, and we praise You. And thank You that Your salvation on the cross is a greater reality than all the pain and sins of everybody around us. Hallelujah! Amen.

26

PRAYING
FOR CONVERSION

This week I met a doctor traveling through Amsterdam airport. I'd met him before in New Zealand. He was abrasive, known for his coarse language. Friends of his prayed for his conversion, and I was asked to go to a tea party where he had also been invited. His friends prayed that the Lord would use me for his conversion. That was the typical New Zealand style. I had previously noticed that they try to organize conversions over there. I was for instance brought into a room to somebody who was a drunkard; meanwhile elsewhere in the church, or in another house, they went down on their knees and prayed that the Lord would use me.

Well, I quite like that. When people are praying the Enemy has little opportunity to interfere when the Lord wants to speak to a soul. That particular day I received a phone call inviting me to go fishing. I really dislike fishing, and I was not at all sorry to say, "I'm afraid I can't, because there is a doctor I need to meet today."

Then the caller said, "But I am the doctor."

"Oh, but that's a different matter," I said. "Then I would love to come." Suddenly fishing became an attractive work environment, giving me at least five or six hours to talk to this doctor. He was very friendly, but there was no sign of conversion.

Afterwards we went to the tea party together and the host asked, "Well, Doctor, have you found the Lord Jesus as your Savior?"

"Oh, no," he replied, "I don't need Jesus. I am quite a decent chap."

The host asked everybody present except the doctor, his wife, and me to go to the other room. I had to laugh when I understood his transparent plan. And I said to the doctor, "All I have to say, I have already said. I will now just show you here in the Bible that they were not my words, but the words you can read here in the Bible."

I read with him from John 1:12 and Revelation 3:20. Then I prayed, "Please, Lord, will You send all the powers away that stand between You and this doctor. Please clear the way." I turned to the doctor. "Now please give your answer to the Lord Jesus."

Very simply he said, "Yes, Lord Jesus, I am a sinner, I accept You as my Savior."

It is strange, but at the moment I thought, is it really that straightforward? I had spent so many hours working towards this and now doubt crept in, but then I was reminded of Paul's words, "Everyone who calls on the name of the Lord will be saved" (Romans 10:13).

The doctor's lifestyle proved that this was a true conversion. The next day he began to talk to his patients about the Lord.

I met a woman in another city who told me about her great need. This doctor had visited her because she was ill. And he had spoken to her about the Lord Jesus and shown her the way. However, she didn't want to and rebelled. But he said, "I will continue to pray for you this evening." She told me that she had wrestled for hours, and at two o'clock in the morning she gave up fighting and said yes to Jesus. It is that important *yes* that gives the angels in heaven great joy.

The next morning the doctor called. She told him what had happened, and he said, "How wonderful that you found the Lord at two o'clock in the morning. I wrestled in prayer for you until that moment. And then the Lord said to me that everything was well."

When I met this woman she was a happy, victorious child of God.

Not only were people so grateful for his spiritual care, but very often when people came with their complaints about pain in the stomach or a swollen knee, and when the doctor felt the need to speak about the Lord, he would say, "I'd rather you told me about the state of your soul. Where will you be in eternity? We will deal with the other matter later." And the curious thing was that many people actually found the Lord in his office.

But one day he was called in by a colleague, who said, "Please stop all that nonsense. All your patients are coming to me and saying, 'If I talk about my headache, that doctor begins to talk about my soul.' If you continue that way you will lose all your customers."

The next day there was only one patient in this faithful doctor's office. But he said, "Lord, if I must suffer poverty with you, there is only one thing I want to do, and that is to obey." The following day there were forty-eight people in his office.

It is truly wonderful to meet a man who is so passionate about the Lord.

Thank You, Lord Jesus, that You can use us all. Some will work for You in a very simple manner, while others have a special way like this doctor. But we thank You that we may all know that we are the branches on the vine. The vine does the work to bring forth fruit. All the branches do is remain connected to the vine. And when we are with You, You prepare us to save others for eternity, which is wonderful, Lord. How easy. Please listen, Lord, to those who are now saying, "I lay my weak hand in Your strong hand, Lord Jesus. Please use me." Hallelujah! Amen.

27

WITNESS!

The Lord Jesus once said, "As the Father has sent me, I am sending you" (John 20:21). Why did the Father send Jesus? To find and make holy what had been lost.

Why are we Christians in the world? To find the lost and send them to the Lord. There is work to be done! We all need to witness; we can all be used by the Lord to bring others to Him. At times it can be quite difficult and today it can even be quite dangerous. In countries where there is no freedom it might mean that we must die for the Lord, which I'm afraid is not unusual. There are many martyrs at present who are taken to prison, or even killed when witnessing for the Lord. But it is so wonderful that the Lord Himself encourages us.

I remember a story I heard from a missionary who went to China. It was still possible, but it was quite dangerous. Somebody asked her, "Aren't you afraid of going there?" And she said, "No, there is only one fear in my heart; it says in the Bible that a kernel of wheat must fall to the ground and die to produce fruit. And now my fear is that I might not be prepared to die."

Yes, we all need to understand that if we lose our lives for the Lord it actually means that we gain them, and that the Lord wants to use us.

I remember once experiencing great encouragement while I was in the concentration camp. It was the moment I was given freedom. There I was, waiting at the gate, and I knew that when the gate opened I would be free. Now it so happened that I had been able to bring the gospel to many people in the concentration camp, which had been wonderful. Many people had found the Lord Jesus. Very many died with the name of Jesus on their lips, and the Lord had used Betsie, my sister, and me to show them the way.

And here I was standing by the gate. My sister had died only two weeks previously. And while I was waiting there, someone came up to me, a friend of mine, and she said, "Corrie, I must tell you something. Today, both Mrs. Was and Mrs. de Mooie died."

I surveyed that cruel concentration camp for the last time and I said, "Thank You, Lord, that You brought me here, that I could be here, if only for these two people whom I know have been saved for eternity. They found the way to You, and You used Betsie and me to achieve it. Lord, if only for these two people all our suffering has been worthwhile, even Betsie's death. To be used to save others for eternity is worth living and dying for."

A while ago I had the opportunity to speak in a prison in New Zealand. I used the text, "You are the light of the world" (Matthew 5:14). Can you say that to criminals in prison? Of course you can! Because any criminals—yes, no matter what kind of sinners they are—coming to the Lord Jesus are cleansed of their sins and have been called to be the light the world. And I love speaking to prisoners about this, because it helps them to see that there is a chance for them. All they have is this incredible inferiority complex, and then suddenly they see that God wants to use them.

When I had finished, one of the prisoners stood up and he said, "Mates, this morning I read in the Bible about three murderers: one was David, the other was Moses, and the third was Paul." Were they murderers? Of course they were—he was right. And he said, "Isn't it wonderful that God can use a murderer and can turn him into a hero like those three people. There is hope for you and me, mates."

He was right. I thought it was a wonderful message he gave us, because yes, Moses, David, and Paul once were murderers, but didn't they become wonderful heroes of God. And you and I can be used too, no matter who we are.

Thank You, Lord, that You want to use us too, no matter what kind of sinners we are. If only we come to You, You will turn us into the light of the world. Hallelujah!

28

THE LEAST OF THESE: PRISONERS

In Matthew 25 Jesus tells us about the final judgment, where he will say, among other things, "I was in prison, and you came to visit me" (verse 36).

"And when did we see you sick or in prison and go to visit you?" some will ask (verse 39).

And Jesus will say, "I tell you the truth, whatever you did for one of the least of these brothers of mine, you did for me" (verse 40).

A prisoner in Germany who had been given a life sentence once wrote me a letter. "Once a month I'm allowed to write, but there is nobody for me to write to in the entire world. May I write to you?" What loneliness! Of course I could say yes and write to the man, but I am a wanderer. Sometimes I work in countries where the post reaches me very slowly or not at all. Moreover, I realized that this man was one of the many lonely people living behind closed prison doors. I took that letter to the Lord and he gave me wisdom.

I then wrote to my magazine *Hallo Freunden*, which I send to my friends in Germany every three months. I mentioned this letter. And I asked if there was anybody, or possibly several people, who would like to correspond with the prisoners. I found a friend who was happy to organize it, and several people joined the plan. Subsequently, I received some wonderful letters.

One lady who had joined the scheme wrote to me, "I was enthusiastic about your plan. I had been praying for years for these people living behind barbed wire, but now I can do something for them. I regularly correspond with six prisoners. I sent all of them the New Testament, and when you write us your newsletter, I send it to them too, which is such a wonderful opportunity to tell them about the Lord Jesus' love for sinners as well as showing them how to start a new life in Him. The work is certainly not in vain."

Yesterday I received a letter from a man who had been in solitary confinement for a long time. He wrote to me, "My life was in ruin, but now I have found the Lord Jesus. And through Him I have received God's grace. I thank Him every day, and I want to be faithful to Him. It is amazing how quickly I learned to believe in the Lord Jesus Christ. That miracle has happened. There I was standing in front of Jesus' cross and suddenly I understood how He also experienced deep suffering and great despair. He can understand me. I want to love Him and serve Him. Suddenly my life was given an aim. I'm writing this to you to show you how happy I am. Please tell me more about the Bible and what it says. The joy Jesus gives us and the salvation of one single human being is worth more than all the wealth in the world. The cross of Jesus was something that was very, very far from me, but now, suddenly, it is very close to me. And it is as if it speaks to me. Yes, I know God can change hearts in each one of us, in the same way as He has changed my heart. I can say this with great certainty; my heart is full of joy."

Someone else wrote, "I accepted Jesus' hand. Each time I receive a letter from you, I forget I am behind bars. When I open my eyes in the morning, I long for Jesus. But I know so little about Him. Tell me more about Him. I thank Him every day. Jesus hears me when I speak to Him."

Can you imagine them sitting there? The man, forlorn in his cell. To hear him talking about Jesus? How it came about? It was an ordinary woman who at first prayed for prisoners and then began to write them letters. Won't the woman rejoice when Jesus says to her, "I was in prison and you visited me there"?

You too should ask yourself if you can do something. You could start in the same way as the woman by first praying for prisoners and then acting. What could you do? Well, maybe write a letter. You will however need wisdom to find out how. It is so wonderful that the Bible gives us such incredible promises. James 1:5 says, "If any of you lacks wisdom, he should ask God, who gives generously to all without finding fault, and it will be given to him."

Just imagine if we were to hear, "I was in prison, and you didn't visit me." Then we will answer Him and say, "Lord, when were you in prison, and when did we not serve you?"

And He will reply, "I tell you the truth, whatever you did not do for one of the least of these, you did not do for me" (Matthew 25:45).

Lord Jesus, I pray You, help us to be faithful to Your Holy Spirit. And help us to be resourceful through Your love. Amen.

29

EVANGELISTS
IN PRISON

I have spoken to prisoners in many countries. During the war I personally experienced what it means to be locked up behind a door that can only be opened from the outside. Maybe that is why I feel so deeply for them. And I have also met many "evangelists" in many prisons.

I'm thinking of this chap in Mexico. He was a serious criminal. He had been given a sentence of eighteen years. Of course you are not given such a sentence for stealing a car. But now something amazing had happened in his life. The Lord Jesus had laid His hands on his life. And once he had prayed, "Come into my heart Lord Jesus," and Jesus came. It says in Revelation 3:20, "Here I am! I stand at the door and knock. If anyone hears my voice and opens the door, I will come in and eat with him, and he with me." And that was what had happened, and he became the evangelist in his prison. When I arrived there, he had already converted half his fellow prisoners.

I hope you will go to heaven, and that I will meet you there. I am convinced that I will be able to introduce you to many passionate evangelists I have met in prisons. Not only that, we will find many prisoners who have found their way to heaven through these men.

Yes, what can God do with you who are listening? What can God do with a sincere sinner who has surrendered completely? Do you want to surrender? Because then miracles will happen, for you are the light of the world.

Thank You, Lord, that You can use sinners, saved sinners, sinners washed clean, cleansed by Your blood, that You can use them as Your light in this dark world. Hallelujah! Amen.

30

LOOKING JESUS
IN THE EYES

I spoke to a kind of chief in Vietnam. His name is Tsau. A whole week I had been talking to his tribe, and he thanked me on behalf of the members of his tribe. He addressed me with the title "aged, aged grandmother." Old age deserves great respect among the members of the Chill tribe and among all the other jungle tribes in Vietnam.

He went on to say, "You have come from far, very far. You are old, very old. You have had to travel a long way to get here, to tell us about the Lord Jesus. Please thank your tribe that they have allowed you to come here."

He gave me a copper bracelet, which was a sign of unity with his tribe. It is also given when tribes are reconciled, once a large debt has been paid completely, also when two people get married. "In your case," Tsau said, "it symbolizes a prayer union. We will pray for you and you will pray for us. That is how in the future we will belong to each other."

And then I asked him, "Do you have a message for my tribe in the Netherlands?"

He waited a moment; I think he was praying. And then he said, "Tell them over there that if somebody doesn't repent of their sins, they will not see Jesus when He returns."

And that is exactly the message I give to you, listeners, on behalf of the Chill tribe of Vietnam, on behalf of Tsau, their spiritual chief. We do not know at which hour or which day Jesus will come, nor do we know of any hour, or any day that He cannot come. If He were to come today, would you be able to look Him straight in the eyes?

The wonderful thing is that we can all be totally prepared if we repent of our sins, because Jesus will forgive us and cleanse us with His blood. A heart cleansed by Jesus' blood will be filled with His Holy Spirit, which will create in us so many wonderful things that we will be prepared. It is a matter of surrendering to Him, of whom the Bible says, "that he who began a good work in you will carry it on to completion until the day of Christ Jesus" (Philippians 1:6).

In Vietnam I also visited the American soldiers close to the frontline in Danang. Can you imagine what it meant for them to have an old lady visiting them? Their wives, their mothers are a long way off in America. One soldier said to another, "She has the same smile as my grandmother." And that is what I felt like, a grandmother visiting her boys who were risking their lives.

At first I had them laughing heartily. Americans have such a wonderful sense of humor. But then I spoke to them very seriously. "Boys," I said, "we all know that you are risking your lives. You might even be killed tomorrow. Are you prepared to look a righteous God in the eyes? Well, it is possible, if you repent of your sins, and take them to Jesus. He wants to forgive you and cleanse your heart with His blood and fill you with His Holy Spirit. He has said, 'Come to Me, and he who comes to Me I will not turn away.'" Many boys, many men came. It is quite well possible that they are now in heaven.

And what about you, my listeners? You might say, "Well, I'm not at the frontline fighting a war; my life is not in danger!" But we all know that one day we will die and then be judged, all of us, whether we want to or not. Are you prepared? Will you be prepared when Jesus comes? If you can say "yes" to that, it is wonderful, but please use your time to show others the way.

It wasn't easy for me to travel through Vietnam and Indonesia. I felt sick due to the climate, and all the misery I saw, and the difficult journeys in the troop aircraft. I even had to return sooner than I had intended.

Eternity is there to be gained or to be lost by each one of us. And if we know Jesus, we know the way and we need to tell others. He is the way, the truth, the life. Tell many others. Let's work as long as it is day, you and me in our own ways. Has the Lord called you to go far away? Then do so! Does he want you to stay? Then be obedient. God can only use us where He calls us. Isn't it wonderful to work for a King who has never lost a battle! And He wants to turn you and me into more than conquerors.

Thank You, Lord Jesus, that we know that You will return again on this earth. Please help us see that we must repent of our sins, so that we will see You, when You come again. Holy Spirit, make us restless today if there is any sin in our hearts of which we have not yet repented. Thank You, Lord Jesus, that You bore the sins of the whole world on the cross, also my sins, and the sins of those who are praying along with me. Thank You. Hallelujah, what a Savior! Amen.

31

HOW TO TAKE STOCK

When I had a watchmaker's shop in Haarlem, I was used to stock-taking at the end of the year. It was something I always enjoyed doing. It was a pleasure to see what beautiful watches and clocks we had in stock, and I could immediately see what was missing. For example, there might not be enough travel alarms and kitchen clocks and we needed to purchase more. It was fun, but it was also very useful doing this kind of work.

Today I would like to begin making an inventory of the stock we have as children of God, which actually is an impossible task. No matter how hard we work, it will only represent a small part of reality. But it is good. We need to live a life rich in Jesus Christ, because the world is so poor without Him.

A Christian needs to be and should be realistic. We can see that the Antichrist is currently marching in, and when we read in the Bible about what we are experiencing now and what we may expect when Jesus returns, it is obvious that many exciting days await us. In Luke 21 the Lord Jesus told us so much and warned us against so many things, and showed us the way with regard to everything that is happening now. We may expect terrible things to happen, even persecution. But the Lord says, Don't be afraid. "When these things begin to take place, stand up and lift up your heads, because your redemption is drawing near" (Luke 21:28).

I once was in a country where oppression was breaking out. Christians were being killed, and suddenly I felt great joy. Never have I opened the Bible with such a feeling of gratitude. I read Romans 8 and 1 Peter 1. What a wonderful abundance of food for the children of God in need! And it is as if we are all standing at the frontline of the battle, not against flesh and blood, but against the evil spiritual powers, against the powers around us. It is a battle which will become fiercer and increasingly serious and where we will absolutely need God's armor, as described in Ephesians 6.

When I was taken prisoner during the war together with my relatives, we had all torn pages from our Bibles and hidden them somewhere under our clothing. When we arrived at the police station, we asked each other, "Tell me, what have you got?" Paul's letters were well represented. Some had taken parts from Ephesians, others from Philippians, letters to the Romans, and also Peter and John's letters. One of us had taken Psalm 91.

One of those days, a brother advised us as Christians to learn the Morse code, because many of us would end up in prison and therefore it would be useful. Well, I don't agree at all. While I was imprisoned during the war, I knew the Morse code, but it didn't really help me. What actually supported me was every text and every Christian song I knew by heart. Learning Bible texts and Christian songs by heart is a preparation which we can all do today.

Don't start with Genesis 1 or Matthew 1 but ask the Lord to guide you through His Holy Spirit when choosing texts to memorize. There is an organization called the Navigators who under God's hand have set up a practical course to learn texts by heart. Yes, we need to learn how to manage the Sword of the Spirit, the Word of God, even if we no longer have the Bible.

What an amazing prospect, what an incredible perspective is given to us in Romans 8. The suffering of today cannot be compared with the glory that is awaiting us. You may see danger and death around you, but the reality is that Jesus lives, and He is with us. "Though you have not seen him, you love him" (1 Peter 1:8). Particularly in the days of great oppression we will be used. We must practice being strong when oppressed, by taking the promises of the Bible seriously.

Today many of God's children are oppressed in a large part of the world. In our days there is darkness over the whole world, knowledge of global despair, a fear of insecurity arising from all visible things. We are shaken by what we see on television and read in the newspapers. It all seems so senseless. Romans 8:22 says, "We know that the whole creation has been groaning as in the pains of childbirth right up to the present time." Verse 19 says, "The creation waits in eager expectation for the sons of God to be revealed." In the Phillips translation it says, "The whole creation is on tiptoe to see the wonderful sight of the sons of God coming into their own."

Who are the sons of God? In Romans 8:14 we read, "Those who are led by the spirit of God are sons of God." We know the secret of God's plan. We can read it in Ephesians 1. And what does this creation see when they see you and me, while it is on tiptoe? Do they see beggars, poor wretches, or do they see the King's children?

Eva von Tiele Winkler once wrote, "We are the King's children, and we possess the key to our Father's Treasury. Those treasures are ready for us, ready for use at any moment in our lives, day and night."

I've only just begun to make an inventory of this treasury.

Lord Jesus, please forgive us that we so often live a life poor in You, while You suffered so heavily on the cross so that we would become the King's rich children. Holy Spirit, open our eyes. Give us a vision, an understanding of our wealth. Please may the creation on its tiptoes see in us exactly what we long to be: victorious, relaxed, rich children of God. Please help us create in the world a sense of holy envy for the wealth which passes all understanding. Amen.

32

BE ALWAYS ON
THE WATCH

In Luke 21:34–35 we read: "Be careful, or your hearts will be weighed down with dissipation, drunkenness and the anxieties of life, and that day will close on you unexpectedly like a trap. For it will come upon all those who live on the face of the whole earth."

I happen to know a very poignant poem written by the preacher Okke Jager:

"Come quickly, Jesus, come!" prays the preacher.
"Yes, Amen," says the farmer. "I will come soon!
But after the harvest, because on my new stretch of
*   land*
I have not yet witnessed any produce."
"Yes, Amen," says the lady, "but do you mind
If I first save up for the fur coat I saw yesterday,
And then wear it when the choir
Sings at a performance for our Christian society?"

"Yes, Amen," says the child, "but not now,
I still need to have my holidays in the forests.
But I will wave, so that you can see me,
When you come to save us during school time."
"Come quickly, Jesus!" prays the preacher.
"But do you mind if I first give that new lecture,
Which I composed for the young people's group
About 'I am sure you will get on well after this.' "
The prayers arrived in heaven.
The cherubim that brought them fell silent.
And Jesus asks: "Do you mind if I leave today?"
His Father sighs: "I'm afraid you will have to wait a
    little longer."

Making a living can keep us so busy that the Sabbath catches us like a noose. Not only do our worries snare us, so do happy expectations: the harvest on the new stretch of land, the fur coat, the holidays, and the lecture on the Bible topic. In themselves they are all good things.

I remember moments during World War II when suddenly there was an immediate threat to our lives during an air raid or in prison. At that moment you saw everything from God's point of view, and it gave you a totally different perspective, because you touched death, and therefore eternity. You saw that small things were small and big things were big. You would see everything in the right proportions.

Seldom have we read with such great interest so many prophecies in the Bible and newspapers side by side, as we did in those days and even today. The Bible says, "When these things begin to take place, stand up and lift up your heads, because your redemption is drawing near" (Luke 21:28). "Be always on the watch, and pray that you may be able to escape all that is about to happen, and that you may be able to stand before the Son of Man" (Luke 21:36).

It might be quite a while before Jesus comes; on the other hand, He might come very soon. Are you ready? It says, "Be always on the watch," even today. The wonderful thing is that we can be ready, you and I, and anybody who belongs to the Lord Jesus. It is a matter of complete surrender to Him who has said, "Come to me and I will give you rest. I will always be with you until the end of the days."

He loves you and me, and that's why I believe He most certainly longs to be with us. He Himself will prepare us for His return. Isn't that wonderful? First Corinthians 1:8 says, "He will keep you strong to the end, so that you will be blameless on the day of our Lord Jesus Christ."

He will do it. And in 1 Thessalonians 3:12–13, it says, "May the Lord make your love increase and overflow for each other and for everyone else, just as ours does for you. May he strengthen your hearts so that you will be blameless and holy in the presence of our God and Father when our Lord Jesus comes with all his holy ones."

My father had those wonderful wise mottos, which he often but never too often repeated to us. I will close this talk with what he said about Jesus: "If He catches hold of us, He holds us tight. If He holds us tight, He leads us on, and when He leads us on, there will be a time when He brings us home safely."

Isn't it wonderful? Lay your hand in His hand, in Jesus' hand.

Thank You, Lord Jesus, for the truth that is so much more wonderful than I can describe. Thank You for bearing our sins and the sins of the world on the cross, and that You want to turn us into God's children—anyone who wishes to accept You. Thank You that You also want to prepare us for Your return by Your Holy Spirit, that You want to make us love each other in abundance today. Thank You that You want to strengthen our hearts. We really need strong hearts in these turbulent times. Thank You that You want to prepare us for the wonderful day when we will see You, when we will see You face to face, no more, no less. Come quickly, Lord Jesus! Amen.

33

NOT FEAR, BUT LOVE

Psalm 46:1–2 says, "God is our refuge and strength, an ever-present help in trouble. Therefore we will not fear, though the earth give way and the mountains fall into the heart of the sea." It says in Luke 21:26 that as one of the signs of the times, "Men will faint from terror, apprehensive of what is coming on the world." Yes, the signs of the times indicate that we can expect Jesus' return very soon. But there is fear in people's hearts. There is good reason to fear, when all the certainties in our lives are shaking as never before. Possessions are insecure. A good position in life? A reasonably high bank balance? It doesn't give any security.

Now that many children of God are reading the Revelation of John and see the signs of the times as an occurrence that has perhaps already started, there is a sort of awakening. In America many Christians are occupied with the near future, when we will not be able to buy or sell if we refuse the mark of the Antichrist (Revelation 13:17). They are creating refuges in houses and farms where food can be cultivated. Is that necessary? I don't know. I believe that God's children will experience great miracles of preservation and deliverance, even if we go through the great oppression. The Bible gives much security both for the present and the future.

"God did not give us a spirit of timidity, but a spirit of power, of love and of self-discipline" (2 Timothy 1:7). Providing room in our hearts for the Holy Spirit is of great importance. Then we will not fear, even if the earth gives way. I have seen how the Lord uses weak people, yes, even children, as channels of streaming, living water in countries where there was, and is, great oppression and persecution of Christians. Their own strength was too weak, but they trusted Him who filled them with the Spirit, not of timidity and fear, but of power, love, and self-discipline. They plainly saw the danger, but also the reality of Jesus' victory.

When I was in a concentration camp, I didn't know in advance that I would be one of the 20 percent of women who got out of the camp alive. I faced death. If you touch eternity like that, you see everything so simply. It was as if I saw the Devil, who was stronger, much stronger than me. But then I looked to Jesus, who is stronger, much stronger than the Devil, and together with Him I am stronger, much stronger than the Devil, and then the fear goes away. Those who are with us are greater and stronger than those who are against us. He who is in us is the strong one, the conqueror. He "who is in you is greater than the one who is in the world" (1 John 4:4).

What we can expect and can already see is that besides fear there will also be much hatred. And now Romans 5:5 is so wonderful: "God has poured out his love into our hearts by the Holy Spirit, whom he has given us." That love is the fixed point in the time to come.

The following story is told of Pastor Wurmbrand, who is a Messianic Jew. One of his fellow prisoners, also a Jew, hated him because he had become a Christian, but he saw that Brother Wurmbrand was full of love and kindness toward the people who tortured him. Then the Jewish man said, "If I get out of here alive, I am going to follow that Jesus whom Wurmbrand confesses, because I can see how there is love in this man toward those who are so cruel to him." He did get out alive and he is now serving Jesus as a real, complete Jew who already knows and follows Jesus, his Messiah.

Human love fails, and will fail. God's love never fails, and we will experience that. And the people with whom we come in contact will experience that because they will see that there is no fear in us, but conquering love, the love of God. And in that love there is no fear. There will no longer be a place for compromise. It will be yes or no. The extremes will reign, either hatred or love.

Religion is no security. The Antichrist will be very religious. A world religion will develop, and he himself will become its god. World history is becoming increasingly chaotic, and it will become even more so. It will be like a hazardous, thick fog. People will live without prospect. The Holy Spirit will clearly show us God's prospect, and we can already see God's plan.

All that we are now experiencing are the signs of the times, clearly foretold in the Bible, pointing toward the great solution, the wonderful future of God's kingdom that will come on earth, which will then be covered with the knowledge of the Lord. As the waters cover the bottom of the sea, the leaves of the tree of life will be used for the healing of the nations.

So there is a future for the nations. The future will be wonderful, the best is yet to come, and you and I may work to hasten Jesus' coming. Be filled with God's Spirit. Then there is love, not fear, the love of God which wins.

Thank You, Lord Jesus, that You put God's love in our hearts through the Holy Spirit which has been given to us. Thank You that that love wins, and remains, and prevents us from fearing, even if the earth gives way and the mountains fall into the heart of the sea. Hallelujah! Come soon, Lord. Yes, come quickly! It is so dark on earth. Prepare us for the great feast. Thank You. Amen.

34

WHEN THE MOUNTAINS FALL INTO THE SEA

In Psalm 46:2 it says, "Therefore we will not fear, though the earth give way and the mountains fall into the heart of the sea." Many mountains around us are crumbling, which makes me all the more grateful that I have the Bible, because the book is full of heavenly certainties that do not fall. You learn to value them more when temporary certainties give way, as for instance during an earthquake.

It is many years ago that I heard the following song for the first time:

I have found the firm ground where I can drop my
  anchor forever.
The foundation in Jesus' blood and wounds, already
  laid before creation.
That foundation will not move, whereas both heaven
  and earth may perish.

We often sang it together; the last verse of the song was so beautiful:

Only on this ground, do I wish to build, as long as I
live on this earth.
This will be the rock on which I build my faith, and I
will rejoice before the throne of the most High
For the salvation prepared for me by Christ, oh won-
derful depth of mercy.

Yes, I do remember that Father enjoyed singing it. Father always was a great help to me. He was a watchmaker, but he was also a great theologian. He read *De Heraut* every week, the weekly paper by Abram Kuijper.

As a child, I asked him, "Daddy, what does it mean to be selected?"

And he said, "The selection refers to the foundation on which I build my hopes; it is not in me, but in God's faith-fulness." If that is how you understand the selection (also called *election*), you will rejoice in it. I've heard so many opinions about selection, originating from the Devil, which he used to undermine and remove our certainty in faith.

"When the mountains fall into the sea." I didn't used to understand those prophecies in the Bible, but they are now so much clearer to me. It is all about what's going to hap-pen at Jesus' second coming. And the days of the Antichrist, they make you tremble. But it all seemed so distant, and I didn't quite understand it. Now I read about the signs of the times in the newspapers. If I'd never believed in the Bible I would have believed what I now read in the newspapers. It makes you feel quite awful when you read about wars, war threats, earthquakes, and other natural disasters. It says in the Bible that people's hearts will shake with fear. Aren't they terrible things that are about to happen? They make you feel sick.

A black minister once said, "When I read a sad book, I always have a quick look at the last page. If it tells you that they will come together and will be happy ever after, then I'm happy to read the rest knowing that all is going to be well.

"And that is exactly what I do with the Bible," he continued. "I look at the last page when I feel a little scared. And then I know that Jesus will come again, He who has promised to make everything new so that the Earth will be covered in the knowledge of the Lord, like the waters cover the sea. The best is still to come. What great comfort."

If you find it a little difficult and frightening, then do read the last page of the Bible. Yes, the best is still to come.

The suffering of today cannot be compared with the glory of what is to come. It is a comfort, but meanwhile there is that certainty today, given to us by the Lord, not a spirit of fear but a spirit of love, strength, and sensibility. Because of the Holy Spirit you need not fear, even though mountains fall into the sea. Be filled with God's Spirit, who shows you that God doesn't have problems, only plans. There never is any panic in heaven. God is faithful; His plans do not fail.

I remember once entering the hall in the concentration camp where my sister Betsie was having a Bible study. She said, "When an architect makes a blueprint of a house, you see all kinds of things on it; a doorstep here, a window there, a roof over there. And that is how God has made a blueprint of my life and yours. Somewhere it was written

'Ravensbrück.' God doesn't make mistakes, even though we don't understand."

Well, I certainly didn't understand when I saw Betsie die. There were still so many things for her to do! There will be a time when we will understand everything in heaven, but now I sometimes understand through the Holy Spirit. I can now already see with regard to Betsie.

In my book *The Hiding Place* John Sherrill describes what I had told him about Betsie. "Over and over again your sister was used by the Lord for me, so that I now can forgive." She showed him that it is the Holy Spirit, who plants God's love in our hearts, which enables me to forgive and love my enemies.

If Betsie had survived, she would never have reached as many people as she has now through her books. In the jungle in Africa I spoke to a woman who lived far away from anywhere. I don't know why, but she lived a very solitary life. And she told me, "Your sister Betsie, I have learned so much from her."

Betsie testified to the wonderful message that God loves this world. That's why we do not have to be afraid, even though the mountains fall into the sea. God loved His world so much that He has given His only Son so that whoever believes in Him will not perish, but will have eternal life. God gave His Son on the cross, which was so terrible! All was lost, wasn't it; what an incredible mountain fell. And that was when something wonderful happened, an answer to incredible despair, the despair of sin. The Savior bore the sin of the whole world, which included my sin and yours.

Thank You, Lord, for doing it for us. Thank You, that You completed it and that we know that You did not only die for us, but that You live for us and that You are with us. And, Lord, we will not fear, even if the earth gives way and the mountains fall into the sea. With You, we will be safe, no matter what happens. Hallelujah! Thank You. Amen.

35

Raised in Paradise

One morning, a woman was reading 1 Thessalonians 4:13 – 18: "Brothers, we do not want you to be ignorant about those who fall asleep, or to grieve like the rest of men, who have no hope. We believe that Jesus died and rose again and so we believe that God will bring with Jesus those who have fallen asleep in him. According to the Lord's own word, we tell you that we who are still alive, who are left till the coming of the Lord, will certainly not precede those who have fallen asleep. For the Lord himself will come down from heaven, with a loud command, with the voice of the archangel and with the trumpet call of God, and the dead in Christ will rise first. After that, we who are still alive and are left will be caught up together with them in the clouds to meet the Lord in the air. And so we will be with the Lord forever. Therefore encourage each other with these words."

While she was reading this, she was made aware of its seriousness in a very special way. Everybody knows that the signs of the times are clear and that major events are imminent, not only those who read the Bible, but anybody who reads the papers. She was so entirely absorbed by her thoughts about Jesus' second coming that she didn't hear a ring of the doorbell. After a while, she suddenly realized and opened the door quickly, holding the Bible in her hand.

"Are you hard of hearing? I had to ring three times," said her milkman.

"Oh, I am terribly sorry," the woman apologized. "No, I am not deaf, but I was reading something in the Bible that was so wonderful that I was oblivious to the world around me. Do you know that it is possible that one day you may come to my door and find that I'm no longer there? And no matter where you ring, wherever Christians live, you will find the house empty. I was just reading that when Jesus returns, we will meet Him in the sky. We will suddenly be changed, and we will see Him face to face. You wouldn't understand why so many people had suddenly disappeared.

"Later, you would hear what had happened and you would ask yourself, 'Why didn't that old woman tell me about this beforehand?' And that is why I am telling you now. Listen, milkman, if you accept Jesus as your Savior, you will be a child of God too. And you will belong to those who will meet Him in the sky."

Irrespective of whether we agree entirely with this old lady's conclusions, or whether we disagree, we do see that she really meant what she said. And she was doing what she had been told to do, which is to look out for Jesus' second coming. Matthew 16:3 says, "You know how to interpret the appearance of the sky, but you cannot interpret the signs of the times." It won't matter at all if we have any money at the time. But it will be very important if we then see the people who meet the Lord with us, those people we have shown the way to redemption. All cleansed hearts present an enormous reservoir of possibilities to God to drink from those wonderful blessings in eternity.

A young girl is dying in a sanatorium in Nortum. She only has a small part of her lungs left. Her breathing is assisted by an oxygen mask. It is a joy to be with her. In her room there is a sense of freedom, which an imminent death can bring when people are prepared to die. She is at the brink of eternity, and it is as if we all have a kind of bird's-eye view of earthly matters. We see reality and earthly matters disappear into the background.

"You know, Corrie," she says, "it will be so wonderful to work in heaven. What will it be like, do you think?"

"I don't know much about it, but I think that there is great activity and without the obstacles we experience on earth. We need to reign over the world with Jesus. We will be so amazingly cleansed and filled with God's Spirit that we will all be able to do the work according to His will. Here on earth we have already experienced Jesus Christ's victory, but the battle against sin still remains. There will be a complete absence of sin in heaven. Do you believe we go to heaven immediately when we die? The Lord Jesus said to the murderer on the cross, 'Today you will be with me in paradise' (Luke 23:43). His body was still on the cross the very moment that he and Jesus entered paradise.

"I believe that anyone who dies in Jesus will immediately be raised in paradise. Paul was longing for this to happen when he wrote in 2 Corinthians 5:8, 'We are confident, I say, and would prefer to be away from the body and at home with the Lord.' He also wrote about the Lord coming for His people when their bodies will be raised. I think that the souls in paradise will be reunited with their heavenly bodies. And that is how we will ascend into the sky, together with the Lord Jesus."

"Corrie," said this young girl, "I know I have eternal life. In John 20:31 it says, 'But these are written that you may believe that Jesus is the Christ, the Son of God, and that by believing you may have life in his name.' But sometimes I am afraid when I think of the moment of death. I have seen so many deathbeds of God's children which were so dark."

"That is why you should now pray that the Lord Jesus will protect you against evil powers when it happens," I told her. "It is a prayer that will always be heard. Turn your eyes to the future. Samuel Rutherford wrote in the sixteenth century, 'Our little inch of time suffering is not worthy of our first night's welcome — home to heaven.' Paul said, 'I consider that our present sufferings are not worth comparing with the glory that will be revealed in us.'"

"Corrie, please read the beginning of John 14 once again."

"Jesus said, 'Do not let your hearts be troubled.' Our citizenship is in heaven. We are heaven dwellers. Our home is there. Death is a tunnel. My mother once said, 'There must be light in the valley of the shadow of death, otherwise there wouldn't be a shadow. Jesus will be our light there.'"

I concluded, "Jude 24 says, 'To him who is able to keep you from falling and to present you before his glorious presence without fault and with great joy.' If He holds on to us He will lead us on, and if Jesus leads us on, there will be a time when He brings us home safely. If we hold His hand, we will not fear, even if the earth gives way and the mountains fall into the sea."

Thank You, Lord Jesus, that there is far more truth in this than we can realize. Oh, isn't it wonderful that we have such a future. And if anybody listening does not yet have part of it, Lord, speak to them and lay Your hand on their shoulders and draw them to You with Your cords of love. Thank You, that I know that You love them so dearly. And that those who come to You will not be sent away. For You have said, "Come, all of you." Hallelujah! Amen.

36

SIGNING UP FOR
THE ARMY OF GOD

D o you want to sign up for the army of Christ Jesus? In 2 Timothy 2:3 we read, "Endure hardship with us like a good soldier of Christ Jesus." Do you want to sign up?

There is an army that is so strong, and so well armed, and with such perfect leadership that victory is guaranteed. It isn't an army fighting for a particular country. It is a global army. Do you know which future is awaiting the world? A kingdom of peace; peace on earth as it is in heaven; our earth covered in the knowledge of the Lord, just as the waters cover the sea; swords beaten into plowshares. Do you want to know more details? Then study the words of the prophets, the words of the Lord Jesus Himself, and those of the apostles, and then the book of Revelation by John.

I heard the following story about Napoleon. A new group of soldiers had signed up and this is how he spoke to them. "Men, if you fight in my army, you can be assured that you will often feel hungry, and there will be no food.

When the weather is poor, there might be no shelter for you. Blood and sweat are awaiting you. But I can assure you one thing: if you fight for me, your life will be devoted to Napoleon, who never lost a battle. Now, just think about it. If you have decided that you want to be a soldier in my army, take one step forward."

He turned around and waited one minute. Then he looked at the young men. There they were standing shoulder to shoulder. He said, "I will give you one more chance. Isn't there one among you who is bold enough? I will wait another minute."

"That's not necessary," one of them shouted. "We have all taken a step forward."

In spite of his dedicated army, Napoleon lost his last battle. But King Jesus will not lose. He was the conqueror, He is the conqueror, and He will be the conqueror. He Himself warned us, "If you follow me, it means taking up a cross. It means dying like a grain of wheat that falls to the ground and dies to bear fruit. If you lose your life for my sake you find it."

Yes, it might mean being a martyr. Peter says in 1 Peter 4:12–14, "Dear friends, do not be surprised at the painful trial you are suffering, as though something strange were happening to you. But rejoice that you participate in the sufferings of Christ, so that you may be overjoyed when his glory is revealed. If you are insulted because of the name of Christ, you are blessed, for the Spirit of glory and of God rests on you."

In a country where it was dangerous to follow Jesus, a young man came up to me. The entire congregation had listened to what the Holy Spirit had told us about following Him. The boy said, "Now I am prepared to live for Jesus, and to die if He wants me to." In the boy's eyes I saw the spirit of glory mentioned by Peter.

The purpose of this global battle we find ourselves in is peace on earth. John wrote about it in Revelation 21:3–4: "Now the dwelling of God is with men, and he will live with them. They will be his people, and God himself will be with them and be their God. He will wipe every tear from their eyes. There will be no more death or mourning or crying or pain, for the old order of things has passed away."

I heard a young man who had read it say, "God wants to plaster the entire universe with photos of his Son." Yes, the boy described it in his peculiar way, but he had well understood what is going to happen in this world.

Isaiah 11:9 says, "For the earth will be full of the knowledge of the LORD as the waters cover the sea." And then there will be peace in Biafra and in Vietnam and there will be the knowledge of the Lord. I haven't been to Biafra; I have been in Vietnam. And oh my dear people, it is so awful. "Well, just stop talking about it," you might say. "We can't do anything about it." We can't? I think we can, if we sign up in the army of King Jesus. Then we will be used to hasten the return of Jesus on earth. He will come again, and He will make everything new, and He will reign as King. That will only happen when the full number of Gentiles enter (Romans 11:25).

The man and the woman, the child you met today, could be the last to enter, and all will be complete. Is it

worth your suffering? Fighting for King Jesus? Just look at
Biafra and Vietnam. Well, of course you could stay closer
to home. There is enough trouble in the Netherlands, and
in your country.

Plowshares, instead of swords. The wolf will dwell with
the lamb. The peace that passes all understanding. Unspeakable love. The fruits of the Spirit everywhere: love, peace,
joy, patience, kindness, goodness, faithfulness, gentleness
and self-control (Galatians 5:22).

*Lord Jesus, come soon, and please do as You prom-
ised. Thank You that You will use all who have just
responded to You: yes, Lord Jesus. Please put me in the
Book of Life and on Your soldiers' roll of attendance.
I want to suffer with the others like a good soldier of
Jesus Christ, no matter where You wish to use me. Hallelujah! Amen.*

37

Marching Orders

Second Timothy 2:3 says, "Endure hardship with us like a good soldier of Christ Jesus." A soldier has to know his instructions. Orders are rules of play. King Jesus said, "As the Father has sent me, I am sending you" (John 20:21). We can learn the rules of play, if we read in the Bible how Jesus did that. A soldier has to obey. Many things go to pieces because your life is not in agreement with God's plan, God's purpose. The word *sin* means "missing the goal." In the Old Testament we read that God came to dwell in the tabernacle because it was built in accordance with His will.

What are we fighting toward? Toward a future where the earth will be covered with the knowledge of the Lord as the waters cover the sea. Here on earth there will be a succession between the King of Light and the Prince of Darkness. The prince of this world, the Prince of Darkness will be dethroned, and King Jesus, the Sovereign of Light, the Messiah will reign.

To serve in the army of the King of Kings, you must come just as you are. Exactly just as you are, with all your sin, your bondage, your ignorance. But you won't stay just as you are. The King himself will make sure that you are trained and that you receive a uniform for your battle against sin which will bring you to victorious ground. Just read about it in Ephesians 6:10–20. The Lord will break your bondage to the past, to people, to habits so that you will be truly free. In John 8:36 Jesus said, "If the Son sets you free, you will be free indeed." Your ignorance will be changed to knowledge. So much so, that you will exclaim, "I can do everything through him who gives me strength" (Philippians 4:13).

How can that be? By opening all the doors and windows, drawers, and wallets to the Lord Jesus. Light came into your room this morning when you opened the curtains. The Holy Spirit is ready like that to come wherever the doors are opened. That commandment, the most wonderful, most joyful commandment in the Bible, "be filled with the Spirit" (Ephesians 5:18), will then suddenly take place.

Jesus wants to live in us through His Spirit, and then the fruit of the Spirit and the gifts of the Spirit will be completely at your disposal. Read it yourself in Galatians 5:22 and 1 Corinthians 12, 13, and 14. Chapter 13 is about God's love, which is poured out into your heart by the Holy Spirit which has been given to you (Romans 5:5). That is a different love than human love, which eventually fails. But God's love never fails.

What armor you receive when you join the army of King Jesus! Do you see that you can't do it, that I can't do it? That it is only Jesus, who in spite of everything already has the power and makes us more than conquerors because He comes to dwell in us through His Spirit.

But why do you sometimes feel so lonely? You feel as if you are far away, that you are on your own in the battle, like the emotions of a soldier who has to go on reconnaissance and feels he is in danger. He is trembling, because he has lost the connection with the army and the general staff. A soldier like that needs a walkie-talkie. Then he is in contact with his superiors, whom he can consult at all times.

Our King never sends us to the front without a walkie-talkie. We are in constant, wonderful contact with Him through our walkie-talkie of prayer. "Pray continually," the Bible says (1 Thessalonians 5:17). That doesn't mean constantly being on your knees, but it is the continuous connection with the Master, right in the middle of the battle of daily work. Sometimes it is just a sigh, an exclamation, a "Lord, thank You that You are with me." "Lord, help me, I'm in trouble!" "I made a mistake, Lord, will You forgive me and help me not to make the same mistake again?" "Praise and thanks to You, Lord. You take such good care of me!" This is how the Master makes you more than a conqueror.

Lord, will You repair our walkie-talkie of prayer where necessary? You are the author and perfecter of our faith. Will You make it a real conversation? It's so nice to spend time alone with You in my quiet time, but also just in the normal course of things. Hear, Lord, whoever says, "I lay my hand in Your hand, Lord, together with You I am more than a conqueror." Hallelujah! Amen.

38

EQUIPPED FOR THE BATTLE

I can see a clear similarity between the life of a child of God today and a soldier at the frontline. We read in Ephesians 6:10–13, "Finally, be strong in the Lord and in his mighty power. Put on the full armor of God so that you can take your stand against the devil's schemes. For our struggle is not against flesh and blood, but against the rulers, against the authorities, against the powers of this dark world and against the spiritual forces of evil in the heavenly realms. Therefore put on the full armor of God, so that when the day of evil comes, you may be able to stand your ground, and after you have done everything, to stand."

An army has its supply officers, also called logistics officers. Just imagine that a soldier came to his officer after a battle and said, "I have not been able to fight. I didn't have any weapons with me. I was so hungry. There was nothing to eat. I saw my comrades bleed to death, but I couldn't do anything to dress their wounds. I didn't even know what the officers expected from me."

Just imagine him saying that to the logistics officer who had provided well for him and who would then say to him, "But there were weapons, weren't there? There was a food supply that I had provided for you, wasn't there? Didn't you have that first-aid box with emergency bandages?"

Imagine that the soldier would reply, "Well, yes, there were bandages, but I used them to clean my shoes." Or that he would say, "I'm afraid I had no idea what to do."

The logistics officer might reply, "I had supplied you with radio communications, a walkie-talkie, which would help you stay in contact with your officers all the time." And that soldier would be severely punished.

Now let us imagine what we would do if we didn't use the supplies the Holy Spirit, our supply officer, gives us for our battle. What are our riches? What is our background? What are our supplies? We have a mighty High Priest on our side and a host of angels. We have the intercession of the Lord Jesus Himself and His Holy Spirit.

Listen, in Romans 8:26 it says, "We do not know what we ought to pray for, but the Spirit himself intercedes for us with groans that words cannot express." And in verse 34, "Christ Jesus, who died—more than that, who was raised to life—is at the right hand of God and is also interceding for us." We have the presence of the Lord Jesus, who said to us, "And surely I am with you always, to the very end of the age" (Matthew 28:20). He stands beside us; He is in us, with us. We are firmly standing on victorious ground. We have a walkie-talkie when the Holy Spirit fills us and turns our prayers into a conversation, a wonderful communion with our King.

Recently, I heard about a little girl in East Germany who was told to write at school, "I don't believe that God exists." She couldn't and therefore she wrote, "I believe that God exists."

The teacher was furious and said to her, "Go home and copy a thousand times, 'I don't believe that God exists.'"

The child came home and said to her mother, "I can't do that. I believe God exists."

Her mother said, "Just write down what you believe."

So the girl wrote down a thousand times, "I believe God exists."

When she had to go to school the following day she was very frightened, but when she arrived in her classroom there was another teacher. That morning her own teacher had been killed in a car accident.

Yes, those who are with us are much stronger than those who are against us. Some time ago when I was on my way to a dangerous place I had a moment of fear, and someone said to me, "When you enter, Jesus will enter." What do you mean? Yes, it is true, because Jesus is in us, and we are in Him. He is in us.

God's provisions, God's logistics are perfect. We need food and the Bible is bread that never goes stale. Heaven and earth will perish, but the Word of God will go on forever. We have the tools, the optical tools, and the communications with HQ. The Holy Spirit gives them to us in His fullness. He turns our prayers into a conversation with the General Staff. You see, our logistics officer can do many things, but if the soldier is disobedient, loses courage, or is frightened and doesn't use the supplies, the officer cannot help him.

I fear that when we hear our personal final judgment we may stand there in shame that we have not lived our life to its fullness. If we were to say, "I was so burdened, so concerned, so restless, so exhausted, so covered in my sins," the answer will be, "Burdened? Hadn't you received my promise: 'Come to me, all you who are weary and burdened, and I will give you rest' (Matthew 11:28)? You were worried? But didn't it say in the Bible, 'Cast all your anxiety on him' (1 Peter 5:7)?"

Imagine we were to say, "I couldn't forgive, I was so bitter; I couldn't burn the engraved sins of others. I couldn't love my enemies, the effort was beyond me." The answer would then be, "Didn't you have a Bible in which it says in Romans 5:5, 'God has poured out his love into our hearts by the Holy Spirit, whom he has given us.' Wasn't there an ocean of God's love for your personal use, every minute of the day and the night?"

Just imagine you were to say, "My sin troubled me so much." Then you will hear, "Don't you have a Bible? Have you never read in 1 John 1:9, 'If we confess our sins, he is faithful and just and will forgive us our sins and purify us from all unrighteousness'? Have you never read in 2 Corinthians 5:21, 'God made him who had no sin to be sin for us, so that in him we might become the righteousness of God'?"

All God's promises are in Jesus. Yes, and amen. And God really meant His promises, which He has given to us in the Bible. Yes, He really meant them. And take the sword of the Spirit that is the Word of God. The sword makes us strong, and the Word of God shows us that we are more than conquerors through Jesus Christ.

Lord Jesus, forgive us that we are often so discouraged, because we look the wrong way. Teach us to accept all the wealth and strength from Your Word, and to enjoy it so that we will truly be Your strong, victorious soldiers. Thank You that we know the best is still to come, and please help us through Your Holy Spirit, that when we look back on our lives we will not be ashamed, because we were too weak in ourselves and not strong in You. Thank You, Lord Jesus, that we can never expect too much from You. Hallelujah! Amen.

39

VICTORY IN BATTLE

At the beginning of World War II there was a young man in one of my clubs who had to serve in the military. He and his father ran a bakery and confectionery. He was a cheerful lad. One night he and the other soldiers were called to march out immediately. "War has broken out," they said. He didn't believe it at all and thought, *It will be another of those boring maneuvers.* So he quickly put some bars of chocolate in his ammunition bag instead of ammunition. That's how he wanted to cheer up his comrades, because they had been called out in the middle of the night. In the fields he realized that it really was war. Fortunately his superiors never heard what he had done.

There is a heavy battle on its way and maybe it has already started: the battle between Jesus Christ and the Antichrist. And each child of God will be at the frontline. Do we want to fight with chocolate or with bullets? "For our struggle is not against flesh and blood, but against the rulers, against the authorities, against the powers of this dark world and against the spiritual forces of evil in the heavenly realms" (Ephesians 6:12). Are we enveloped in the power of Jesus Christ? Or do we want to fight with chocolate bars of idealism, philosophy, humanism, and religious piety, our own endeavors and efforts?

Jesus said in Acts 1:8, "You will receive power when the Holy Spirit comes on you." The armor in Ephesians 6 does not cover our backs. God cannot use deserters. Paul says in 2 Timothy 2:5, "Similarly, if anyone competes as an athlete, he does not receive the victor's crown unless he competes according to the rules." When Jesus bore the sin of the world on the cross at Golgotha, including your sin and mine, He beat the Devil. That is where Satan was broken. Jesus had twelve disciples: eleven were martyrs; one was a deserter and traitor.

Paul said to Timothy, "Endure hardship with us like a good soldier of Christ Jesus" (2 Timothy 2:3). Strength is given to us through the Holy Spirit. And the Bible says, "Be filled with the Spirit" (Ephesians 5:18), which means not only do I have the Holy Spirit, but also does the Holy Spirit have me? The Bible is full of promises about strength and victory. It speaks of more than conquerors, about the strength of God's might.

But now we need to live a rich life in Jesus Christ and fight valiantly in Him. What is the use of possessing millions and living like a bum? We need to live out a lifestyle that befits our wealth. A Christian's lifestyle should be one of victory, of joy and abundance, a life that has been given to us through Jesus Christ from God's fullness. We should not rely on our capacities, but on God's capacities. We shouldn't draw from our limited resources, but from his immense power.

The Bible speaks of being made new. It requires a conversion, being born again. The Lord Jesus said, "I tell you the truth, no one can see the kingdom of God unless he is born again" (John 3:3). At birth a baby is weak and dependent; it needs to grow. We don't want to remain dependent, weak children of God. We should cash the "checks" written in the Bible in our names. Unspeakable riches, a love that passes all understanding await you. The man made new must live inside you and find a way.

Yes, but which way? Jesus Christ is the way. It means that the self-centered life becomes a Christ-centered life. Paul calls the self-centered life the old self. We need to get to know our old self, and that meeting is not always a pleasant one. Do we want to repair the old self? We might try to build a neat facade to protect a shabby interior and give it a fresh coating of paint and washed curtains. But whoever wants to be converted needs to open the door and let the Lord Jesus in, and show Him everything without hiding anything. It is called a sense of sin. And it is different from the knowledge that you might have committed a sin. Whoever has experienced this meeting and wants to accept the consequences will find a new form of life. He takes on the new self; he is a new creation.

Thank You, Lord Jesus, that You want to do it. I can't, the old self in me is so stubborn, so strong, but it is wonderful that You make the new self, that You want to live in us through the Holy Spirit. And that we therefore stand on victorious ground in our battle against the many evil powers. Hallelujah! What a Savior! Amen.

40

CITIZENS OF HEAVEN

Philippians 3:20–21 says, "But our citizenship is in heaven. And we eagerly await a Savior from there, the Lord Jesus Christ, who, by the power that enables him to bring everything under his control, will transform our lowly bodies so that they will be like his glorious body."

In being born again, we are born into the family of God, and there the Lord Jesus gives us eternal life. He makes us citizens of the kingdom of heaven. We already have that eternal life now, if we are children of God, whether we are aware of it or not.

My father was very aware of it. If, for example, we had an unexpectedly happy evening through a blessed visit, a conversation, or beautiful music, he often said, "That was a very small foretaste of heaven, of the joy that we will experience there." But he also saw everyday life in that glow of eternity. He said, "My name is on my watchmaker's shop, but God's name should actually be on it, because I am a watchmaker by the grace of God."

I worked with my father for twenty-five years, and I saw that he was first a child of God, and then a businessman, and that he led a holy life in the workshop and the shop. Being citizens of a kingdom in heaven doesn't make us unworldly, because it says in Psalm 24:1, "The earth is the LORD's, and everything in it, the world, and all who live in it."

But if I was just a citizen of the world, I would run the risk of becoming desperate; I can see that all around me. Atheism is marching across the entire world. The unclean is becoming more and more unclean. People say that there will be a nuclear war in the future. But that is the amazing thing. We know that the earth is the Lord's. You can't understand all this with your logical mind; it's the foolishness of God which can only be understood by faith.

I saw an awful part of a Nazi concentration camp, where bodies had been laid on the ground in a wash house. Those who wanted to wash themselves had to step over them. There I saw a little bit of the citizenship of the kingdom of heaven. It was the dead face of my sister, Betsie. There was a heavenly peace and joy to be seen.

As the Bible tells us, we are citizens of the kingdom of heaven. "In my Father's house are many rooms," the Lord Jesus once said, "I am going there to prepare a place for you.... And if I go and prepare a place for you, I will come back and take you to be with me that you also may be where I am" (John 14:2–3). Yes, from there we expect the Lord Jesus Christ as Redeemer. The signs of the times of the second coming of He who "will transform our lowly bodies so that they will be like his glorious body" (Philippians 3:21) are very clear, so it could happen very soon.

We know something of Jesus' body from what the Bible tells us. He could enter through closed doors. We read that about the gathering of the ten, and later eleven apostles. He ate and drank; He could travel great distances; He could make himself invisible. Just read the story of the road to Emmaus. But the most important thing was that Jesus' glorious body had no sin, illness, or death, and that He will transform our lowly bodies so that they will be like His glorious body. The purification already starts here, and so it must.

When John speaks of the second coming, he says, "Everyone who has this hope in him purifies himself, just as he is pure" (1 John 3:3). How? Looking to Jesus makes us mirrors of His love. In 2 Corinthians 3:18, Paul says, "And we, who with unveiled faces all reflect the Lord's glory, are being transformed into his likeness with ever-increasing glory, which comes from the Lord, who is the Spirit."

When the Indian missionary Sadhu Sundar Singh was in England and rang at the door of a house somewhere, a little girl said, "Mummy, it's Jesus standing there!" Sadhu had looked to Jesus so much that he had received something of Jesus' appearance. I saw him myself when I was young, and I can imagine that Jesus looked like that.

Yes, perhaps we can accept it of someone like Sadhu. But this text in Philippians 3:21 is written about you and me. Is that possible? By the power that enables Him to bring everything under His control. There is a resurrection power, which is so strong that Jesus can bring everything under His control, and that power is strong enough to change us small, insignificant, sinful people so that we will be like Jesus' glorious body. He will bring everything under His control; that is a wonderful future. Philippians 2:10–11 says, "At the name of Jesus every knee should bow, in heaven and on earth and under the earth, and every tongue confess that Jesus Christ is Lord, to the glory of God the Father."

Will He be your judge or your Savior? Do you know that you are holy, set apart for such a wonderful reality? Paul writes, "I know whom I have believed, and am convinced that he is able to guard what I have entrusted to him for that day" (2 Timothy 1:12). And you and I can say that too.

Thank You, Lord Jesus, that You have made us citizens of heaven and that You will transform our lowly bodies so that they will be like Your glorious body. Thank You, Lord, that the best is yet to come. Amen.

ACKNOWLEDGMENTS

Special thanks to:

Rinse Postuma, director, Trans World Radio voor Nederland en Belgie (Netherlands and Belgium), for special permission to transcribe and translate Corrie's Dutch audio messages into English and for allowing the proceeds from this book to benefit TWR's international ministry;

Claire L. Rothrock, Trans World Radio-Europe, the Netherlands, for championing this project, researching TWR's audio archives, and overseeing, coordinating, and assisting with the transcription and translation process from Dutch to English;

Cor Weeda of Trans World Radio voor Nederland en Belgie, for bringing to our attention the existence of the never-before-translated audio messages;

Clara M. van Dijk, retired, Trans World Radio voor Nederland en Belgie, for championing the initial vision and being a strong advocate for publishing the Corrie messages in English;

Rosemary Mitchell-Schuitevoerder, for her work as the primary translator;

Dieteke Visser and Uyen Do, for their work in transcribing the audio materials into written form;

Hella van den Broek, manager of Attract Uitzendbureau, for her assistance in identifying qualified transcribers and ensuring the completion of the transcription process in a timely manner;

Hans van der Steen, retired director, Trans World Radio voor Nederland en Belgie, who initially brought Corrie ten Boom's radio ministry to life by working directly with her to coproduce her broadcasts, and without whom the messages in this book would not have existed;

Tom Watkins, Trans World Radio-Americas, for initiating and providing general oversight of this project, and for editing the final manuscript.

Share Your Thoughts

With the Author: Your comments will be forwarded to the author when you send them to *zauthor@zondervan.com*.

With Zondervan: Submit your review of this book by writing to *zreview@zondervan.com*.

Free Online Resources at

www.zondervan.com/hello

 Zondervan AuthorTracker: Be notified whenever your favorite authors publish new books, go on tour, or post an update about what's happening in their lives.

 Daily Bible Verses and Devotions: Enrich your life with daily Bible verses or devotions that help you start every morning focused on God.

 Free Email Publications: Sign up for newsletters on fiction, Christian living, church ministry, parenting, and more.

 Zondervan Bible Search: Find and compare Bible passages in a variety of translations at www.zondervanbiblesearch.com.

 Other Benefits: Register yourself to receive online benefits like coupons and special offers, or to participate in research.